THE YEN/DOLLAR AGREEMENT

POLICY ANALYSES IN INTERNATIONAL ECONOMICS 9

THE YEN/DOLLAR AGREEMENT: LIBERALIZING JAPANESE CAPITAL MARKETS

Jeffrey A. Frankel

INSTITUTE FOR INTERNATIONAL ECONOMICS
WASHINGTON, DC
DECEMBER 1984

DISTRIBUTED BY MIT PRESS
CAMBRIDGE, MASSACHUSETTS, AND LONDON, ENGLAND

Jeffrey A. Frankel, Associate Professor, Department of Economics, University of California at Berkeley, was a Visiting Fellow at the Institute for International Economics in October and November 1984. From August 1983 to August 1984, he was a Senior Staff Economist, Council of Economic Advisers, Washington.

The author wishes to thank Ken Froot for extremely capable research assistance and to thank for comments and suggestions: Gerard Caprio, Dorothy Christelow, William Dellal, Richard Freeman, Shafiqul Islam, Takatoshi Ito, Steven W. Kohlhagen, Ichiro Otani, Charles Pigott, Gary R. Saxonhouse, and three referees, all of whom looked at earlier drafts; Koichi Hamada, Yuzo Harada, Yuzuru Ozeki, Kermit Schoenholtz, and other participants at an August 17–18, 1984 symposium at the Ministry of Finance in Japan; Ulrich Baumgartener, C. Fred Bergsten, I. M. Destler, Sena Eken, Robert Fauver, Stephen Marris, John Williamson, and other participants at an October 4, 1984, seminar at the Institute for International Economics. J.A.F.

INSTITUTE FOR INTERNATIONAL ECONOMICS
C. Fred Bergsten, *Director*
Kathleen A. Lynch, *Director of Publications*
Michele McCord, *Business Manager*

The Institute for International Economics was created, and is principally funded by, the German Marshall Fund of the United States. This publication is part of the overall program of the Institute, as endorsed by its Board of Directors, but does not necessarily reflect the views of individual members of the Board or the Advisory Committee.

Library of Congress Cataloging in Publication Data

Frankel, Jeffrey A.
  The Yen/Dollar Agreement: Liberalizing Japanese Capital Markets.

  (Policy analyses in international economics; 9)
  "December 1984."
  Bibliography: p. 73
  1. Investments, American—Japan.   2. Banks and banking, American—
Japan.   3. Capital market—Japan.   4. Japan—Foreign economic relations—
United States.   5. United States—Foreign economic relations—
Japan.   I. Title.   II. Series.
HG5772.F73   1984   332.6'7373'052   84-27842
ISBN 0-88132-035-8 (Institute)
ISBN 0-262-56034-8 (MIT Press)

Contents

PREFACE *page ix*

1 PROLOGUE *page 1*

2 JAPAN-US TRADE AND THE ALLEGATION THAT THE YEN IS ARTIFICIALLY UNDERVALUED *page 5*

The Japan-US Trade Imbalance *page 5*
Is the Yen Undervalued, or the Dollar Overvalued? *page 9*
Have the Japanese Acted to Weaken the Yen? *page 16*

3 LIBERALIZATION OF INTERNATIONAL CAPITAL FLOWS *page 19*

The Japanese Liberalization of 1979–80 *page 19*

New Measures to Liberalize Capital Outflows *page 26*

Samurai Bonds *page 27*
"Administrative Guidance" Restricting Overseas Lending by Japanese Banks *page 28*
Sales in Japan of Foreign Commercial Paper and CDs *page 28*
Deposits of Residents in Overseas Financial Institutions *page 29*

New Measures to Liberalize Capital Inflows *page 29*

"Designated Company" System for Direct Investment *page 29*
Real Estate *page 30*

Direct Measures for Japanese Government Borrowing in the United States *page 30*

"Nakasone Bonds" *page 30*
Issue in New York of Government Agency Bonds *page 31*

4 INTERNATIONALIZATION OF THE YEN *page 31*

The General Issue of "Internationalization" *page 32*

Use of the Yen as a Reserve Currency   *page 34*

Use of the Yen for Denominating and Financing Trade   *page 36*

"Real Demand" Rule for Forward Exchange Market   page 39
Banker's Acceptances   page 39
Preferential Import Financing by the Bank of Japan   page 40

Use of the Yen in the Euromarket   *page 40*

Euro-yen Bond Issues by Nonresidents   page 41
Euro-yen Bond Issues by Residents   page 41
Withholding Tax on Earnings from Eurobonds Issued by Residents
   page 42
Participation of Banks in the Euro-yen Market   page 43
Offshore Banking Facility in Tokyo   page 43

5   TREATMENT OF US FINANCIAL INSTITUTIONS IN JAPAN
   page 44

Establishment of Foreign Branches in Japan   page 45
Limits on Swap Loans   page 46
Management of Trust Funds   page 46
Dealing in Japanese Government Bonds   page 47
Membership in the Tokyo Stock Exchange   page 47

6   LIBERALIZATION OF DOMESTIC CAPITAL MARKETS   *page 47*

Measures to Liberalize Domestic Markets   *page 49*

Bank Certificates of Deposit   page 49
Government Securities   page 49
Households' Deposits   page 51

The Order of Liberalization   *page 51*

**7   PUBLIC REACTION TO THE LIBERALIZATION OF OCTOBER 1983–
MAY 1984   *page 53***

Reactions in the Media   *page 53*
Reactions in the Market   *page 55*

8 THE CURRENT ACCOUNT AND SAVING IN JAPAN, AGAIN
page 60

9 CONCLUSIONS *page 64*

APPENDICES *page 67*

A Excerpts from House Testimony, Under Secretary Beryl W. Sprinkel
   page 69
B Excerpts from Murchison-Solomon Executive Summary *page 70*
C Excerpts from Presentation by Secretary Donald T. Regan *page 71*

REFERENCES *page 73*

TEXT TABLES

1 Nominal and real interest differentials *page 11*
2 Japan's financial transactions with rest of world *page 20*
3 Openness of Japanese financial markets: Euro-yen interest rate (three-month), less gensaki rate *page 23*
4 Openness for five countries: Eurocurrency interest rate (three-month), less money market rate *page 24*
5 Share of national currencies in total identified official holdings of foreign exchange, end of years, 1976–83 *page 36*
6 Percentage of Japanese trade invoiced in yen *page 37*
7 Reaction of spot dollar/yen rate to news *page 57*
8 Reaction of one-year forward dollar/yen rate to news *page 59*

TEXT FIGURES

1 Nominal currency values *page 12*
2 Real currency values *page 14*
3 Interest rates on the yen *page 22*

Preface

The negotiations between the United States and Japan during 1983–84 over liberalization of the Japanese capital markets, the subject of this study, were a unique event in the history of international economic policy. Pressure from one country on another to liberalize its markets is common in trade policy, but never before has one country so pressed another to integrate its financial markets with the rest of the world and to internationalize its currency. Moreover, the negotiations were launched personally by President Ronald Reagan and Prime Minister Yasuhiro Nakasone from their summit meeting in Tokyo in November 1983 in an effort to avert intensification of economic conflict between their nations. And when the agreement was concluded six months later, officials of the US Treasury Department labeled it "historic."

The question addressed in this study is whether the Yen/Dollar Agreement achieved the basic purpose set out by the American and Japanese heads of government—to reduce, if not eliminate, the severe misalignment in the exchange rate relationship between the dollar and the yen. That misalignment has been a prime contributor to international imbalances of unprecedented magnitude in 1984: a global current account deficit of about $100 billion for America and a global current account surplus of almost $40 billion for Japan, and a bilateral Japanese surplus with the United States now expected to reach $35 billion. These disequilibria raise major questions for the economies of both countries, for stability of the international monetary and trading systems, and for overall (as well as "purely economic") relations between the United States and Japan.

The Institute is particularly pleased to publish a study of this topic from the unique perspective of Professor Jeffrey A. Frankel. A widely respected analyst of exchange rate determination, Professor Frankel was involved personally in the official US planning for the negotiations with Japan during his tenure (August 1983–August 1984) as Senior Staff Economist responsible for international economic policy at the Council of Economic Advisers, and observed the talks from close range. His subsequent analysis of the effort was completed while in residence at the Institute as a Visiting Fellow in October and November 1984.

This study is part of an ongoing program at the Institute connected with the United States–Japan Consultative Group on International Monetary Affairs. The group is a small task force of private American and Japanese experts, launched by the Institute in early 1984 under the sponsorship of the

ix

United States–Japan Foundation. Its goal is to work jointly on the wide range of international financial issues which have become so critical to the two countries, in both their bilateral relationship and their responsibilities for stability of the global monetary system. The group considered the issues covered in this study at its first meeting, in March 1984, and will discuss them further (along with other major international financial topics) at upcoming sessions in January and April 1985.

The Institute for International Economics is a private nonprofit research institution for the study and discussion of international economic policy. Its purpose is to analyze important issues in that area and to develop and communicate practical new approaches for dealing with them.

The Institute was created in November 1981 through a generous commitment of funds from the German Marshall Fund of the United States. Support is being received from other private foundations and corporations, and the Institute now seeks to broaden and diversify its financial base. The Institute is completely nonpartisan.

The Board of Directors bears overall responsibility for the Institute and gives general guidance and approval to its research program—including identification of topics that are likely to become important to international economic policymakers over the medium run (generally, one to three years) and which thus should be addressed by the Institute. The Director of the Institute, working closely with the staff and outside Advisory Committee, is responsible for the development of particular projects and makes the final decision to publish an individual study.

The Institute hopes that its studies and other activities will contribute to building a stronger foundation for international economic policy around the world. Comments as to how it can best do so are invited from readers of these publications.

C. FRED BERGSTEN
Director
November 1984

1 Prologue

In late September of 1983, Lee Morgan, chairman of Caterpillar Tractor, came to Washington. He visited top officials at the White House, Treasury, Council of Economic Advisers, and other agencies. As he went, he left two gifts. The first was a copy of a new study entitled "The Misalignment of the US Dollar and the Japanese Yen: The Problem and Its Solution" by David Murchison and Ezra Solomon. The second was a toy Caterpillar tractor—made in West Germany. (The Executive Summary of the Murchison-Solomon report is reproduced in appendix B.)

Morgan spoke both as a representative of the Business Roundtable and as chairman of a US maker of construction equipment engaged in intense worldwide competition with a Japanese company (Komatsu). The US trade balance was deteriorating rapidly, particularly in manufactured goods. The bilateral trade deficit with Japan was alleged to account for nearly half of the total US deficit.[1] The principal cause of the imbalance was a misalignment in the yen/dollar exchange rate. It was frustrating for a company like Caterpillar to make the difficult effort of bringing its production costs under control, only to be overwhelmed by a weakening of the yen against the dollar that made price competition with the Japanese impossible. The yen had depreciated against the dollar due to capital outflow from Japan. The capital outflow, he argued, was in part the effect of a number of Japanese government policies.

The Japanese were alleged to follow policies that make it difficult for foreigners to hold yen, that discourage capital inflow by keeping domestic interest rates artificially low, that restrict foreign direct investment in Japan, and that reduce demand for the yen by avoiding its use as an international transaction currency. Morgan urged the Washington policymakers to progress from "benign neglect" of the dollar to a "positive exchange rate policy." His suggested remedy was a list of measures Japan would be encouraged to take to liberalize Japanese financial markets and internationalize the yen. The effect would be reduced Japanese capital outflow, a strengthened yen, and an improved US trade position. The ideal occasion to press the plan on the Japanese was President Reagan's November 1983 trip to Japan.

---

1. Murchison and Solomon (1983, p. 2). In fact the correct figure for 1983 was 31.3 percent of the total US trade deficit.

1

Morgan had been to Washington before, but his audience had not been entirely sympathetic.[2] *A Treasury study had found that the Japanese government had not been intervening in international capital markets to keep the yen undervalued. Indeed Beryl W. Sprinkel, Under Secretary of the Treasury for monetary affairs, had testified to that effect as recently as April 21, 1983. (An excerpt appears in appendix A.) Furthermore, Treasury had been more inclined to attribute the rapidly rising US trade deficit to the nascent US economic recovery, rather than to exchange rate factors.*

But that September, Morgan's message received a more enthusiastic reception in some quarters. The administration had always been committed in principle to free international capital markets. A campaign to induce the Japanese to "open up" their financial markets seemed a natural extension of the effort already underway to induce them to open up their goods markets. It particularly appealed to the "take charge" orientation of Treasury Secretary Donald T. Regan. Furthermore, an excellent case could be made that movement in the direction urged by Morgan could be traded off domestically against strong election-year pressures for protection of US business from Japanese imports.

An extended list of measures to urge on the Japanese was drawn up in early October, and the matter was given high priority when the President visited Japan. For Prime Minister Yasuhiro Nakasone, to whom successful management of the US relationship was politically crucial, some concessions in the area of financial markets must have seemed easier at the margin than settling thorny longstanding issues, such as US pressure for the Japanese to import more beef, citrus, metallurgical coal, natural gas, tobacco products, computer software, and telecommunications equipment, and also easier than suffering the consequences of exacerbated protectionist resistance to Japanese exports in the United States. Furthermore, the Japanese financial system had in any case already been evolving in the desired direction, and for good reasons.

The result was a November 10, 1983, agreement between Regan and Japanese Finance Minister Noboru Takeshita, in which Japan agreed to eight specific measures regarding financial market liberalization. To monitor progress in implementing these measures, and to pursue additional measures, Regan and Takeshita set up an ad hoc Yen/Dollar Working Group cochaired by Under Secretary Sprinkel and Vice Minister of Finance Tomomitsu Oba.

The US government, inside the subsequent six meetings of the Working

---

2. Rowley (1983) and Katz (1984).

Group as well as outside, took the attitude that the Japanese had yet to make substantive concessions. When Secretary Regan visited Tokyo on March 24, 1984, his tone was hostile. (Some of his remarks appear in appendix C.) By playing hardball, the US side in the end won most of what it had sought. The Yen/Dollar Working Group reached agreement on further Japanese liberalization measures and submitted its report on May 29, 1984.[3]

The measures that the Japanese were encouraged to take fell into four categories:

● liberalization of Japanese barriers against the inflow and outflow of capital

● "internationalization" of the yen

● more favorable treatment of US banks and other financial institutions wishing to conduct business in Japan

● deregulation of domestic Japanese capital markets, allowing more interest rates to be market-determined rather than fixed by the government.

The US side got almost all it asked for, at least in the first three categories. Only in the fourth category will Japanese policy continue to differ greatly from the US ideal, at least until a phased schedule of deregulation is completed. There are presumably limits on how far one sovereign country can push another in internal economic affairs.

In the judgment of the author and most other American economists who have looked at the issue, the liberalization of Japanese capital markets is clearly very good for the Japanese economy.[4] It will allow Japanese households

---

3. When it became more evident that the fruits of the US campaign would not include a major impact on the value of the yen, some Treasury officials sought to deny that the exchange rate had ever been the primary motivation. Following this logic, the many explicit statements by top officials (see for example, paragraph 2, appendix C) could conceivably have been merely for public consumption. Other motives indeed entered, such as a genuine belief in the efficiency of free capital markets. But two pieces of evidence attest to the importance attached by Treasury to the exchange rate objective. First, the name of the Sprinkel-Oba committee was, after all, the "Working Group on Yen/Dollar Exchange Rate Issues." Second, some very busy senior US officials spent much valuable time, on airplanes to Tokyo and elsewhere, to pursue this enterprise. This suggests a certain sense of urgency, beyond the priority attached to encouraging France, for example, to liberalize its own highly regulated financial system in the cause of free markets.

4. For example, Pigott (1983), Niskanen (1983, p. 74), Saxonhouse (1983b, p. 293), Freeman (1984), Council of Economic Advisers (1984), and *World Financial Markets* (June 1984), pp. 2, 11. For an in-depth Japanese study favorable to liberalization, see Sakakibara and Kondoh (1984).

to earn a fair rate of return on their saving, and it will help allocate saving efficiently among sectors of the Japanese economy, or allocate it abroad if that is where the rate of return is highest.

One could perhaps argue that the system whereby the government channels cheap credit to various industries has served Japan well in the past.[5] But increased flexibility of interest rates was in any case made inevitable by the events of the last 10 years. The 1970s saw a decrease in the rate of investment in Japan and a corresponding emergence of substantial government deficit financing, the continued trend of increased interdependence among Japan and its trading partners, and the sensitivity of inflation rates worldwide to supply shocks. More recently there has been a higher level of real interest rates worldwide as well, and a desire on the part of the Japanese government to minimize the differential in real interest rates vis-à-vis the United States, so as to avoid further weakening of the yen against the dollar. All of these factors, as well as continued technological innovation in telecommunications and banking,[6] have undermined the viability of a system that in the past fixed interest rates at artificially low levels.

Unfortunately, however, the main original motivation for the US campaign for liberalization of Japanese financial markets—the supposed effect on the yen exchange rate—was based on questionable economic logic. It is by now often conceded that the liberalization will have little effect on the value of the yen in the short run; the payoff is supposed to occur in the long run. However, it is not even clear that the effect, to the extent there is one, will be in the desired direction. Economic theory suggests that liberalization of international capital flows and improved treatment for US financial institutions in Japan will, if anything, have a downward effect on the value of the yen, under the circumstances of the 1980s. This is especially true to the extent that they take place in advance of domestic deregulation measures. An

---

5. Saxonhouse (1983b, pp. 294–95) draws a distinction between the hypothesis that the Japanese government has successfully allocated capital among specific sectors and the hypothesis that it has followed macroeconomic policies to keep the economywide cost of capital low, thus raising the rate of aggregate capital stock growth. With regard to the first hypothesis, Saxonhouse (1983a, pp. 15–19; 1983b, pp. 276–77) argues that the Japanese system of allocating capital among sectors at best reproduces the signaling and resource allocation functions of American markets in venture capital and equity, in contrast to the conventional view represented by Iwata and Hamada (1980). With regard to the second hypothesis, Saxonhouse (1983b, p. 295) admits the possibility that Japanese policymakers have deliberately stimulated growth by keeping interest rates low. Here, Horiuchi (1984) questions the conventional view.
6. See Suzuki (1984) for an account of financial innovation in Japan.

increased worldwide demand for the yen as a transaction and investment currency would indeed have an upward effect on its value, but this is less a matter of steps open to the Japanese government to internationalize the yen than of decisions beyond Japanese control made by private agents.

The remainder of this paper is organized as follows. Section 2 briefly reviews trade issues between the two countries and the overall argument that the Japanese have artificially kept the yen undervalued. Sections 3 through 6 consider, respectively, the four categories of measures that make up the liberalization effort. Section 7 looks at the public reaction to the 1983–84 events, in the media and in the markets. Section 8 examines the broader argument that Japanese policy raises its current account surplus, even if not necessarily via the exchange rate. Nine conclusions are summarized at the end.

2   Japan-US Trade and the Allegation that the Yen Is Artificially Undervalued

This study is not intended to be a comprehensive analysis of the yen/dollar exchange rate issue or US-Japanese trade imbalances. These issues are only relevant insofar as they relate to the 1984 liberalization of Japanese capital markets and the role played by the US campaign launched in October 1983. Nevertheless, it may be useful to set the stage by discussing the larger context, relations between the two countries regarding international trade and payments, that gave rise to the campaign.

The Japan-US Trade Imbalance

Bergsten (1982) points out that we are now experiencing the third episode of major economic conflict between the United States and Japan since 1970. As with the first two episodes, in 1970–71 and 1977–78, the most visible cause of the 1981–84 episode is an upsurge in the US bilateral trade deficit with Japan. The bilateral deficit reached a record $19.3 billion in 1983 and is headed for a 1984 level as high as $35 billion. As with the earlier episodes, the most damaging effect is an upsurge of US protectionism.

In analyzing the Japanese and US trade balances, it is useful to distinguish longstanding structural trends from more recent macroeconomic factors. We will begin with the most comprehensive magnitude, each country's current account balance, which adds services and transfer payments to the merchandise trade balance. In 1983, Japan ran a current account surplus of $24 billion, equal to 1.8 percent of GDP. The Organisation for Economic Cooperation and Development (OECD) forecasts that in 1984 it will be 2.4 percent of GDP. Part, but not all of these surpluses, are structural.

A country's current account balance indicates its changing investment position vis-à-vis its trading partners. A current account deficit means that foreigners are accumulating net claims on assets located in the domestic country. Countries with profitable investment opportunities, such as South Korea, Hong Kong, Taiwan, Singapore, and other rapidly industrializing countries, are normally in this situation, borrowing savings from abroad to finance their development. For the first 20 years after World War II, Japan was also in this situation.

A current account surplus means that the domestic country is accumulating net claims on assets located abroad. Because Japan is now a capital-rich country with a high saving rate, it has normally been in surplus since 1965, lending its savings to other countries where they can earn a higher rate of return. Despite sharp movements into deficit after the 1973 and 1979 oil shocks, Japan's current account averaged a surplus equal to 0.55 percent of GNP from 1971 to 1981. Such a surplus was on the same order of magnitude as Germany's. It would translate into about $7 billion in 1983.

But by now Japan can be considered to have completed the rest of its adjustment to the higher real worldwide price of oil. In August 1984, in an official Economic White Paper, the Economic Planning Agency of Japan estimated the structural current account surplus to be about 1 percent of GNP, explaining about half of the 1983 current account surplus of $24.2 billion. Yoshitomi (1984a, p. 17; 1984b, pp. 5–6) offers estimates of the structural current account surplus that stretch the range upward from the official number: 1 percent to 1.5 percent of GNP, or $12 billion to $18 billion as of 1983.

Japan runs an international deficit in services, particularly transportation, tourism, licensing, royalties, and management fees. As a matter of arithmetic, it must run a surplus in merchandise trade that is bigger than its overall current account balance, in order to pay for the net imports of services. In 1983, Japan's deficit in services and transfers was about $12 billion, very close to the 1971–81 average as a share of GNP. Yoshitomi's estimates thus imply a structural merchandise trade surplus of $24 billion to $30 billion.

The upper end of this range corresponds roughly to recent levels of the US bilateral deficit vis-à-vis Japan. This correspondence is a coincidence. But it does dramatize the fact that the United States is taking a larger share of the Japanese surplus than one would expect merely from the size of the United States in the world economy, a circumstance that has two causes, one structural and one macroeconomic.

The reason for the structural Japan-US bilateral surplus is basic. Japan has few natural resources and depends on imports for its supply of primary products: agricultural products and, especially, oil and other mineral fuels. In 1971–81 its average deficit in primary products equaled 6.6 percent of GNP, which would translate into $76 billion as of 1983. Because Japan must earn the foreign exchange to pay for the oil by exporting other goods, it habitually runs a large surplus in manufactured goods. This surplus averaged 8.2 percent of GNP in 1971–81, equivalent to $95 billion as of 1983. Saxonhouse (1983b, pp. 272–74, 286–95) finds empirically that the standard Hecksher-Ohlin theory of comparative advantage explains well the pattern of Japanese trade, in particular that Japan's low endowment of natural resources and high endowment of high-quality labor explains the high manufacturing component of its exports. He finds it possible statistically to reject the hypothesis that sector-specific Japanese policies were at work, in all but 17 out of 109 commodities, representing a much smaller percentage of Japan's trade than was the case for France or Italy.

Japan's need to export manufactured goods to pay for imports of primary products explains why the bilateral surplus with the United States is so large. If the United States were willing to sell Alaskan oil to Japan, the bilateral trade imbalance would be reduced.[7] As it is, Japan buys its oil elsewhere,

---

7. Japan does import many of its agricultural products from the United States; indeed Japan is the largest customer of US agriculture. Still, liberalization of Japanese nontariff barriers to the imports of such goods as beef and citrus products would increase agricultural imports. Some liberalization took place in connection with the Reagan-Nakasone summit of November 1983.

Liberalization benefits both Japanese consumers and US farmers. However, it does not benefit the US manufacturing sector. The greater volume of imports into Japan tends to depreciate the yen against the dollar, making it even more difficult for Americans to compete against Japanese manufacturers. In the long run, the yen depreciates until Japan generates the increased trade surplus in manufactures necessary to pay for the increased trade deficit in agriculture. Japanese

running a large bilateral deficit with the Organization of Petroleum Exporting Countries (OPEC). And Europe normally runs a bilateral deficit with the United States. It is as if the United States sells to Europe in order to be able to buy from Japan, Japan sells to the United States in order to be able to buy from OPEC, and so forth around the circle of trading partners. The important point is that it is neither necessary nor desirable for any two countries' bilateral trade to be in balance, any more than it is necessary or desirable for an auto manufacturer to be in bilateral balance with its steel supplier, or a household with its plumber. One looks at the overall balance of a household, company, or country, not at bilateral balances, to see if it is earning more—from all its trading partners together—than it is paying out.

Currently the United States is, of course, earning far less overall than it is paying out. It is no longer making up for its imports from Japan by selling to Europe; in 1983, bilateral US-European trade was virtually in balance for the first time. Indeed, over the last three years, the US deficit has deteriorated with all major parts of the world but OPEC. The overall US trade deficit registered a record $61 billion (on a balance of payments basis) in 1983 and is expected to reach as high as twice that level in 1984. We now turn to the macroeconomic component of the trade imbalance.

The US trade deficits are not primarily structural. They are in part attributable to a large loss in net exports to financially troubled Latin American countries, and in part to the rapid pace of the US recovery in 1983 and 1984, which has led to rapid growth in imports. But conventional calculations suggest that by far the largest contributor to the deterioration in the US trade deficit is the very large appreciation of the dollar.[8] As of October 1984, the appreciation has been 69 percent against an average of 10 trading partners' currencies, weighted by their shares in world trade, relative to the average for 1980. (Other calculations that give more weight to the currencies of Canada and Japan produce smaller magnitudes.) Very little of the dollar

protectionism, like protectionism in the United States and anywhere else, distorts the pattern of trade in a way that hurts both trading partners on net; but it is not a major source of the Japanese trade surplus. These points are made by Saxonhouse (1983b, p. 285) and the Council of Economic Advisers in the 1983 and 1984 *Economic Report of the President*.

8. Of the estimated $60 billion deterioration in the US trade deficit between 1983 and 1984, roughly two-thirds can be attributed to the real appreciation of the dollar over the preceding several years (at an annual rate of 13 percent), and roughly one-third to the relative cyclical position (real growth of 6 percent in the United States and 3 percent among its trading partners). This calculation assumes conventional estimates of trade elasticities for relative prices (1.3) and incomes (2.0). The base is imports of $260 billion and exports of $200 billion.

appreciation has been offset by a more rapid increase in trading partners' price levels than in the US price level. In other words, the dollar has appreciated not only in *nominal* terms but also in *real* terms. The real appreciation since 1980 comes to 63 percent. As a result of this loss in US competitiveness on world markets, exports are much lower, and imports much higher, than they would otherwise be. Thus, Murchison and Solomon (pp. 15–16) are correct in emphasizing the damage that the exchange rate is doing to American manufacturers.

It is difficult to be certain about the causes of the dollar appreciation, let alone to quantify them. Exchange rate movements are notoriously difficult to explain. The large reduction in actual and expected inflation achieved in the United States since 1980 is no doubt an important cause in itself. In response, the demand for money has increased in the United States, and so the equilibrium value of the dollar has risen. Nominal interest rates have also declined somewhat in the United States since 1980, but by much less than the decline in expected inflation. Indeed, if the nominal interest rate had declined by the same amount as the expected inflation rate, then the real interest rate would not have changed. In that case, although we would have our explanation for the nominal appreciation of the dollar, we would not have an explanation for the real appreciation of the dollar.

But the increase that did take place in the real interest rate, and in particular the differential vis-à-vis real interest rates in other countries, provides the explanation we need. Table 1 shows the US real interest rate as compared to Japan and Germany. The short-term real interest differential vis-à-vis Japan is about 4 percent and the long-term real interest differential 3 percent. The higher real interest rate in the United States has attracted an inflow of capital, causing the dollar to appreciate in real terms. The real appreciation has been greater than seems likely to be sustainable in long-run equilibrium, although as of late 1984 it still had shown no signs of reversal.

Is the Yen Undervalued, or the Dollar Overvalued?

It is useful to inquire into the meaning of the words "undervalued" and "overvalued." The US Treasury maintains that the dollar is not overvalued. The word means very different things to different people.[9]

---

9. Six distinct definitions of overvaluation and undervaluation are discussed in Frankel (1984) with reference to the recent appreciation of the dollar. Islam (1983) considers the same issues, with particular reference to the yen. Williamson (1983) seeks to estimate the magnitude of the misalignment of the dollar, yen, and other currencies.

On one extreme, a narrow definition of overvaluation could apply the term only if the total demand for the currency at the going exchange rate is less than total supply; in other words, foreign exchange markets do not function efficiently. But in the world of 1980s communications technology, it is difficult to believe that transaction costs are important enough to separate investors from their desired portfolios to any significant degree. Neither are government capital controls important enough to do so, at least for the United States. (We will be considering this issue for Japan in the next section.) Thus, the dollar cannot be overvalued in this sense.

A second definition would consider a currency overvalued if *private* demand for the currency at the going exchange rate is less than total *private* supply. In other words central banks are buying up the difference, supporting the value of the currency through foreign exchange intervention. The dollar is certainly not overvalued in this sense either. It is administration policy to intervene only when necessary to calm disorderly markets. On those rare occasions since 1980 when the US authorities have intervened, and more common occasions when foreign central banks have intervened, it has been to sell dollars, not to buy them. In general, the value of the dollar is whatever the market says it is. This is what Treasury spokesmen mean when they say the dollar is not overvalued.

At the opposite extreme, some people might define a currency to be overvalued whenever its value exceeds purchasing power parity (i.e., when it has appreciated in real terms), or when the country is running a current account deficit. Both definitions clearly apply to the dollar in 1984. Alternatively, a currency could be defined as overvalued if it is expected to depreciate in the future (in nominal or real terms) as reflected, for example, in the (nominal or real) interest differential. A positive interest differential is the compensation that investors demand before they will willingly hold a currency that is expected to depreciate in the future. This too is the case with the dollar, as shown in table 1.

Some Americans, reasoning backward from the large bilateral deficit vis-à-vis Japan, have claimed that the yen/dollar exchange rate is particularly far out of line, and that the Japanese government bears some of the responsibility. Do the Japanese keep the yen artificially undervalued? The question can be broken into two parts:

- Is the yen undervalued?

- Do the Japanese authorities follow policies to reduce the value of the yen?

TABLE 1   **Nominal and real interest differentials**
(percentage per annum)

Source (Observation date)	Variable	Dollar	Yen	Dollar − yen	Mark	Dollar − mark
			Short-term			
World Financial Markets (end Aug.)	One-year Euro-currency interest rate	12.6	6.5	6.1	6.2	6.4
IMF (Sept.)	One-year lagged CPI inflation rate	4.2	2.3	1.9	2.3	1.9
	One-year real interest rate	8.4	4.2	4.2	3.9	4.5
			Long-term			
Economist (Sept. 14)	Government bond yields	12.3	7.1	5.2	7.7	4.6
Data Resources, Inc. (Sept. 11)	Inflation forecast through end 1986	4.8	2.6	2.2	2.8	2.0
	Long-term real interest rate	7.5	4.5	3.0	4.9	2.6

The Murchison-Solomon report was an improvement over some earlier American pronouncements[10] in that it did not claim that the yen was more "undervalued" than European currencies.[11] Indeed it would be difficult to do so. Already by mid-1983 several studies had pointed out that, by a variety of measurement methods, the nominal and real depreciation of the yen against

10. For example, an earlier report from Caterpillar Tractor explicitly argued that the problem was a weak yen, not a strong dollar.
11. The report instead made references to "the misalignment between the dollar and other currencies, most importantly the yen" (Murchison and Solomon 1983, p. 3).

FIGURE 1 **Nominal currency values**

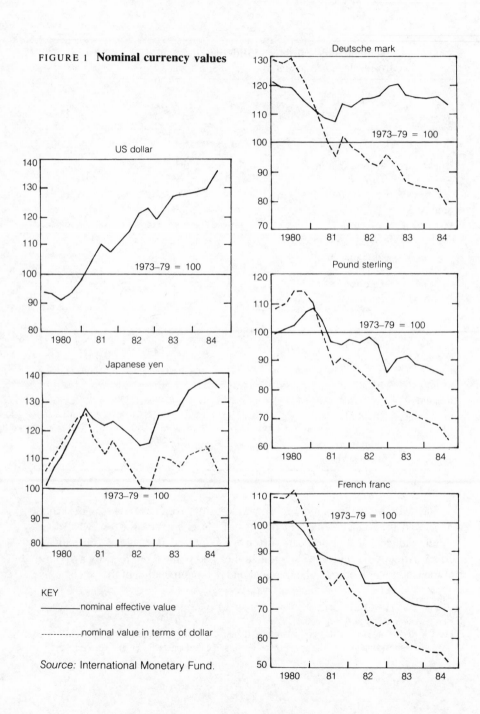

KEY

————nominal effective value

--------------nominal value in terms of dollar

Source: International Monetary Fund.

the dollar had been significantly less than the nominal and real depreciation of the German mark, French franc, and other European currencies.[12] Since then, the yen has continued to hold steady against the dollar, while the European currencies have continued to depreciate (figure 1). In fact, as of October 1984, the yen had actually *appreciated* 4 percent against the dollar, relative to the 1973–79 average, while the mark had depreciated 27 percent against the dollar. In fall 1984 the yen hit all-time highs against the European currencies.

To determine to what extent the yen/dollar problem is a yen problem and to what extent a dollar problem, the value of each currency must be computed in terms of a weighted average of trading partners, rather than examined in terms of bilateral exchange rates. Such a computation shows that, while the effective exchange values of the European currencies have steadily decreased over the last four years, the effective exchange value of the yen has increased. (These are the heavy lines in figure 1 and use IMF trade weights.) Indeed if one takes as the basis of reference the average of the entire period since currencies began to float in 1973, the value of the yen has increased as much as the value of the dollar.

A similar comparison holds in real terms (figure 2). While US manufacturers have sharply lost price competitiveness relative to trading partners, and German and French manufacturers have gained price competitiveness, the Japanese have fluctuated in the middle. The point is not that US manufacturers have not been hurt by exchange rate movements in their efforts to compete against the Japanese; they clearly have been hurt badly. The point is, rather, that the primary problem is with the strong appreciation of the dollar and the roots of that appreciation within US economic policy, not with the yen or Japanese economic policy.[13]

As we have seen, the dollar is strong against the yen because of the net capital flow out of Japan and into the United States, largely in response to

---

12. Council of Economic Advisers (February 1983, pp. 65–66); Sprinkel (April 1983, p. 2; reproduced in appendix A); Williamson (September 1983); and Frankel (1984, pp. 97–99).

13. Islam (1983, p. 56), based on a variety of calculations, also finds that "the yen's weakness against the dollar (or, more precisely, Japan's gains in competitiveness against the United States) reflects the overall strength of the dollar rather than any overall weakness of the yen." Similarly, Freeman (1984, p. 16) finds "on a weighted-average basis the yen, on balance, has strengthened slightly from its average level in 1980, suggesting that the present yen-dollar exchange rate relationship is more a matter of dollar strength than it is yen weakness." And Niskanen (1983, p. 72): "The so-called yen problem is best described as a dollar phenomenon, maybe even a dollar problem."

FIGURE 2 **Real currency values**

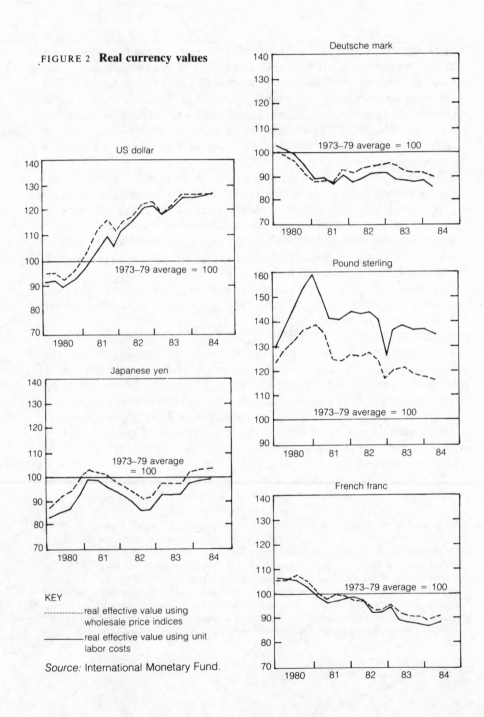

KEY

- - - - - - - - real effective value using
 wholesale price indices

——————— real effective value using unit
 labor costs

Source: International Monetary Fund.

the higher real rate of interest in the United States.[14] Why is the real interest rate higher in the United States than in Japan? The real interest rate can be viewed as being determined by the balance of savings and investment. The rate of national saving, both private and public, is much lower in the United States than in Japan. In 1982, gross national saving in the United States was only 15.9 percent of GDP, as compared to 30.8 percent of GDP in Japan.[15]

In the past, the high level of investment in Japan made good use of the high level of saving. In the 1970s, as the rate of investment declined, the rate of government saving, which is the budget surplus, was steadily reduced. This was a deliberate policy to absorb the excess of private saving and ensure adequate aggregate demand. However, after the budget deficit reached 5.5 percent of GNP in 1978, the Japanese concluded, rightly or wrongly, that it was out of control and began to tighten fiscal policy. Between 1980 and 1984, the Japanese structural deficit was cut by an estimated 2.8 percent of GNP.

Meanwhile, in the United States, national saving was declining, from 15.4 percent of GNP in 1980, to 13.2 percent in 1983. Since 1982, most components of saving, especially retained corporate earnings and the surpluses of state and local governments, have increased in the course of the strong US recovery, returning to their 1980 levels by mid-1984. However, the structural federal budget position has continued to deteriorate. The increase in the cyclically adjusted federal budget deficit between 1980 and 1984 has been about 2½ percent of GNP. Even if the surpluses of state and local governments are added in to make the numbers comparable with Japan's, the US structural government budget declined by an estimated 1.1 percent of GNP between 1980 and 1984.[16] While Japan has moved to reduce government dissaving, the United States has been moving in the opposite direction.

---

14. It should be noted that in recent years, especially 1983, real interest rates in Japan have by many measures been higher than those in European countries, and second only to real interest rates in the United States. See, for example, Islam (1983). This is consistent with the observation that the yen has been stronger in value than the European currencies, and second only to the dollar.

15. OECD *Economic Outlook* (July 1984), p. 155.

16. The US national saving numbers are from the Council of Economic Advisers. The cyclically adjusted federal budget deficit is from the Department of Commerce. Both countries' structural deficits including state and local government are from the OECD *Economic Outlook* (July 1984), p. 28.

To the credit of Morgan and Murchison-Solomon (p. 21), they recognize
the role of high US federal budget deficits and real interest rates in attracting
capital and driving up the value of the dollar. The Japanese delegation in the
negotiations did not hesitate to raise the budget deficit issue either. The
Regan-Takeshita announcement in November 1983 and the Yen/Dollar
Working Group Report in May 1984 both contained promises on the US side
to seek to reduce the deficit. But as a practical matter, the wishes of Japan,
like the wishes of Europe, are not considered important in US government
deliberations with respect to macroeconomic policy.[17]

Have the Japanese Acted to Weaken the Yen?

The most obvious way for the Japanese authorities to keep the yen at a lower
level than it would otherwise be ("undervalued," in the second definition,
above), would be to intervene in the foreign exchange market, selling yen
and buying dollars. The Bank of Japan in fact practiced such intervention in
1976 and 1977, in an eventually futile attempt to dampen what was at that
time a strong appreciation of the yen against the dollar.[18]

The Japanese authorities have long followed a policy of trying to moderate
fluctuations in the exchange rate, known as "leaning against the wind."[19]
Since April 1981, a period when the dollar has been strong against the yen,
the Japanese have at times sold dollars, most recently in the last week of
June 1984. The intervention does not appear to have been effective in raising
the value of the yen against the dollar, but it has operated in the desired
direction, and has been considerably greater in magnitude than intervention
by US monetary authorities.

Monetary policy is generally considered to be a more powerful determinant
of exchange rates than is foreign exchange intervention that is "sterilized"
so as to have no effect on the money supply. In recent years, Japanese

---

17. Even on issues of more obviously legitimate concern to Japan, such as unitary taxation, if
a neutral observer applied the same standards to judge whether the United States side has lived
up to commitments made in the November announcement and May report, that the Treasury
has applied to the Japanese side, the neutral observer might find that the US side is at best only
now beginning to follow through.

18. See Bergsten (1982, p. 1066) for an account of the 1976–77 episode.

19. Danker (1983); Sprinkel (1983, p. 1; reproduced in appendix A); Council of Economic
Advisers (1984, pp. 67–68); Hama (1984, pp. 5, 8); GAO (1984, pp. 15, 21).

authorities have followed a tighter monetary policy than they otherwise would have, with the aim of supporting the value of the yen. In 1982, when nominal interest rates were declining in other countries to reflect reduced worldwide inflation rates, the Bank of Japan delayed even a half-point reduction in the discount rate until October 1983.[20]

Because Japanese foreign exchange intervention and monetary policies have acted to support the yen in recent years, those who wish to argue that the authorities in Tokyo manipulate the value of the yen downward have been obliged to rely on arguments about capital controls. Murchison and Solomon (pp. 21–22) charge, "policies that restrict purchases of yen by foreigners, whether by prohibiting such purchases, making them difficult to obtain or by making them undesirable, depress the yen vis-à-vis the dollar." Similarly, James Abegglen (1983, p. 14) of the Boston Consulting Group writes, "Because [Japan's] trade surpluses can be offset by controlled outflows, the Finance Ministry if it chooses to can determine the range in which the yen will trade."[21]

As we will see in the following section, the Japanese authorities did indeed in the 1970s maintain restrictions against capital inflow. But, like the foreign exchange intervention, the policy with respect to the restrictions attempted to lean against the wind. From 1979–83, when the wind was blowing the other way, the remaining Ministry of Finance restrictions and administrative guidance were more a force reducing capital outflow, and therefore reducing the depreciation of the yen, than the reverse.

In the fall of 1982 several congressional committee chairmen asked the US General Accounting Office (GAO) to investigate charges that the Japanese government had been manipulating the value of the yen downward (and to study more general exchange rate questions as well). The GAO report (p. 21), ultimately published on April 20, 1984, "found no support for charges that the Japanese government deliberately engineered an undervalued yen to

---

20. Ito (1983, p. 25); GAO (1984, p. 19); Hama (1984, pp. 5, 8); Freeman (1984, p. 15); McKinnon (1984, p. 63); OECD (1984, pp. 26, 57, 63–64).

21. As cited by Rowley. Abegglen (March 1983, p. 3) provides a novel argument that the Ministry of Finance depresses the value of the yen by restricting capital *outflow*:

If the yen and Japanese lenders were part of the world money market, the current level of interest rates in Japan could not be maintained; the current very substantial undervaluation of the yen could not be continued. Interest rates would have to be raised instantly and drastically to prevent a run from the yen. The resulting higher interest rates in Japan would bring about quick yen revaluation in the marketplace.

enhance its international competitiveness." In particular, "Available evidence suggests that administrative guidance has been used to support the yen when it was weak as well as to counter the yen during periods of yen strength."[22]

To recapitulate the arguments made in this section, the large bilateral trade surplus that Japan runs vis-à-vis the United States is not due to Japanese government intervention in its capital markets. There is a structural bilateral surplus that is attributable to the current account surplus normally run by high-saving countries like Japan, and to the fact that Japan must generate much larger surpluses in manufactured goods to pay for deficits in services and primary products. Beyond the structural factors, the 1984 bilateral surplus is unusually large due to powerful macroeconomic forces. Because of a recent tightening of fiscal policy in Japan and a loosening in the United States, real interest rates have risen in the United States relative to Japan. The increase in US real interest rates has attracted a capital flow across the Pacific, causing the dollar to appreciate against the yen and, especially, against other currencies. The Japanese government however, far from seeking to magnify the fall in the dollar/yen rate since 1980, has sought to dampen it, through foreign exchange intervention, monetary policy, and its remaining capital controls.

We turn now to consider the four categories of liberalization measures urged on the Japanese authorities by the US government in the year beginning October 1983. In each case we will try to evaluate the likely effect on the yen/dollar exchange rate. Our analytical framework for doing so will be the traditional balance of payments view of exchange rate determination: if a given measure would at the initial exchange rate lead to an increased Japanese payments surplus (whether on merchandise trade account, services account, or capital account), then under the floating exchange rate system it will lead to an immediate appreciation of the yen, to equilibrate the balance of payments. We adopt this common-sense framework rather than more theoretical views of exchange rate determination such as the monetary approach, because under the latter most of the liberalization measures considered would have no effect at all, and we wish to consider the rationale for the yen/dollar

---

22. Freeman (1984, p. 15) observes, "The majority of the most prominent international capital controls and guidance that have been in effect recently on international transactions have been directed at restraining capital outflows—presumably to prevent any further decline in the yen." Other studies with similar findings are Pigott (1983, p. 39); Council of Economic Advisers (1984, p. 68); Hama (1984, p. 7); and Eken (1983, pp. 12, 37).

campaign on its own terms. (It must be acknowledged that of the theories that economists have proposed, none explains exchange rate fluctuations empirically as well as we would like.)

3   Liberalization of International Capital Flows

The first category of measures, dealing with the Japanese treatment of capital flows from or to foreign countries, as distinct from the treatment of domestic borrowing or lending in Japan, is at the heart of the confusion regarding the exchange rate effects of the entire effort.

The Japanese Liberalization of 1979–80

The postwar international economic system, established at Bretton Woods in 1944, did not incorporate a presumption, analogous to the one incorporated regarding international trade, about the undesirability of government intervention in international capital markets. A general postwar trend toward greater capital mobility was temporarily reversed in the 1960s when the United States and other countries adopted controls on international capital movements as part of the effort—ultimately unsuccessful—to preserve the system of fixed exchange rates.

After the Bretton Woods system was abandoned in 1973, the United States, Canada, Germany, Switzerland, and (in 1979) the United Kingdom, one by one removed their capital controls. As recently as early 1979, Japan still retained formidable barriers to both inflow and outflow. For example, foreigners were not allowed to hold many types of Japanese financial instruments. Since real interest rates in the late 1970s were very low in the rest of the world, the controls resulted in a lower net flow of capital into Japan and a lower exchange value of the yen than would have otherwise obtained. This was undoubtedly the intent; the yen hit an all-time high against the dollar in 1978 and the Japanese were trying to dampen its appreciation.

TABLE 2   **Japan's financial transactions with rest of world**
(million dollars)

	1974	1975	1976	1977	1978
Current account balance	− 4,693	− 682	3,680	10,918	16,534
Long-term capital (net)	− 3,881	− 272	− 984	− 3,184	− 12,389
Change in assets	4,063	3,392	4,559	5,247	14,872
Change in liabilities	182	3,120	3,575	2,063	2,483
Short-term capital, and errors and omissions (net)	1,735	− 1,722	228	9	1,805

Source: OECD *Economic Survey* (1984, p. 94); 1984 figures from *The Japan Economic Journal,* November 27, 1984.

When the yen depreciated rapidly in 1979, the Japanese moved quickly to remove controls on capital inflow, making it possible for foreigners to hold Japanese securities: yen-denominated bonds, gensaki (a three-month repurchase agreement), yen-denominated certificates of deposit (CDs), and "impact loans," (foreign currency loans to Japanese nonbank residents).[23] Indeed capital inflow was at times actively promoted. The Foreign Exchange and Foreign Trade Control Law of December 1980 formally established a presumption that international capital flows are permitted, in place of the previous presumption that they were not.

The de jure liberalization took place de facto as well. The rate of accumulation in Japanese (gross) liabilities to the rest of the world, especially long-term liabilities, increased sharply in 1980 (table 2, line 4). This is direct evidence that foreigners were able to invest in Japan. But the table also shows that the rate of accumulation of Japanese claims on the rest of the world increased sharply in 1981 and continued to grow thereafter. On balance, capital has been flowing out of Japan since 1981.

The net capital outflow—the source of the yen's weakness vis-à-vis the dollar since 1980—is attributable to a number of factors such as the high real interest rates in the United States, as we saw in the preceding section.

---

23. The relaxation of controls at first applied only to short-term impact loans, but in 1980 was extended to medium- and short-term loans (OECD, 1984, pp. 56, 60, 78).

1979	1980	1981	1982	1983	Jan.–Sept. 1984[a]
− 8,754	− 10,746	4,770	6,850	20,799	31,436
− 12,618	2,394	− 6,449	− 14,969	− 17,700	− 43,521
16,294	10,817	22,809	27,418	32,459	
3,676	13,211	16,360	12,449	14,757	
4,710	− 44	− 465	3,148	2,078	

a. Annual rates.

But one factor that allowed the outflow to take place is precisely the partial liberalization in 1980. The fruits of that episode would not make one optimistic that the 1984 liberalization will have an upward effect on the value of the yen.

One cannot always rely on capital flow data to reach conclusions regarding the degree of openness. For example, in the theoretical state of perfect capital mobility, there is a potentially infinite volume of capital flow ready to respond if the rate of return in one country is excessively high; yet, once any such opportunities for excess profits have been arbitraged away, no large ex post flows need be observed.

A more reliable market test is a comparison of the domestic Japanese interest rate with the offshore, or Euro-yen, interest rate. Figure 3 shows the gensaki interest rate in Tokyo and the Euro-yen interest rate in London.[24] That the Tokyo rate exceeded the London rate in 1978 is clear evidence that capital controls were operating to reduce capital inflow into Japan. Otherwise, foreign residents would not have been willing to hold Euro-yen when a higher interest rate was available in Japan.

In 1979, the differential between the gensaki and Euro-yen rates dropped sharply. In fact, the London rate exceeded the Tokyo rate during most of 1979 and 1980, although the differential was relatively small. This is evidence

24. Such a chart was, to my knowledge, first used by Otani and Tiwari (1981). Similar charts appear in Ito (1983), Council of Economic Advisers (1984), and Freeman (1984).

FIGURE 3   **Interest rates on the yen**

Annual percentages

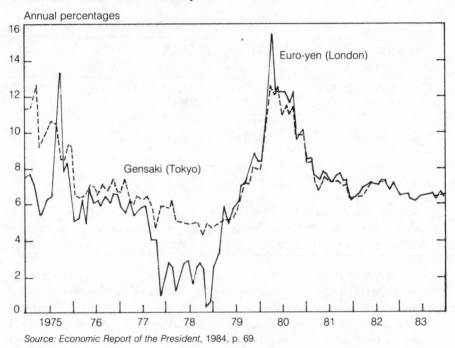

Source: Economic Report of the President, 1984, p. 69.

that Japanese controls on capital inflow were liberalized more quickly than controls on capital outflow. If some barriers to capital outflow had not remained, Japanese investors would not have been willing to hold assets in Tokyo when a higher interest rate on comparable yen securities was available in London. The implication is that those capital controls that remained were more a force keeping capital inside the country than outside, and thus more a force keeping the yen value up than keeping it down.[25]

Table 3 documents the change in the interest differential resulting from

---

25. The Euro-yen–gensaki differential was also positive in late 1973 and early 1974, indicating that capital controls were used to inhibit outflow as in 1979–83, but was much larger in magnitude, reaching almost 30 percent at one point (Ito, 1984, pp. 8–9). This was a time of strong pressure for capital outflow and yen depreciation as a result of the 1973 oil shock.

TABLE 3   Openness of Japanese financial markets: Euro-yen interest rate (three-month), less gensaki rate

	Before liberalization Jan. 1975 to Apr. 1979	After liberalization May 1979 to Nov. 1983
Mean	−1.84	+0.26
Mean absolute value	2.06	0.31
Mean square	6.67	0.29
Variance	3.29	0.22

Note: Weekly data, observed at end of week.
Source: Morgan Guaranty.

the 1979 Japanese decision to allow foreigners to hold gensaki.[26] The mean changed from negative to positive. More significantly, the magnitude of the differential fell sharply by any of three measures. By 1983, the gensaki rate was so close to the Euro-yen rate as to suggest that Japanese markets for short-term negotiable instruments were fully integrated into world capital markets. As of October 1984, the differential for the yen was as small as for any of the major currencies, small enough to be within the margin of transaction costs in the Euromarkets (the bid-ask spread).

The comparison with the European currencies is a particularly revealing one in light of Secretary Regan's statements comparing Japan unfavorably with the United Kingdom, France, Germany, and Switzerland (appendix C). Table 4 presents statistics on the differential between the Eurocurrency interest rate and domestic interest rate, for the yen and four European currencies. For 1979–84, the United Kingdom showed the smallest differential by all measures, which is perhaps an unsurprising consequence of using London as the observation post for the world Eurocurrency market. Germany comes in second (assuming we care only about the magnitude of the differential and not the direction). Japan comes in a respectable third. Indeed, during a recent seven-month period, chosen so as to be able to include Swiss data, Japan

26. May 1979 is the date at which nonresidents were first allowed to hold Japanese securities, like gensaki and CDs, with flexible market-determined interest rates (Ito, 1983, p. 10; Danker, 1983, p. 89; Sakakibara and Kondoh, 1984, pp. xxix, 83). The ban on acquisition of yen-denominated bonds by nonresidents was abolished in February (OECD, 1984a, p. 78).

TABLE 4   **Openness for five countries: Eurocurrency interest rate (three-month), less money market rate**

| | Statistics for Mar. 2, 1979 to May 4, 1984 | | | |
	Japan	United Kingdom	Germany	France
Mean	+0.226	+0.100	−0.276	+2.715
Mean absolute value	0.331	0.172	0.305	2.778
Mean square	0.337	0.070	0.151	20.848
Variance	0.286	0.060	0.074	13.477

| | Statistics for Oct. 7, 1983, to May 4, 1984 | | | | |
	Japan	United Kingdom	Germany	France	Switzerland
Mean	+0.053	+0.109	−0.041	+1.813	+0.116
Mean absolute value	0.101	0.114	0.103	1.813	0.161
Mean square	0.015	0.017	0.020	5.071	0.036
Variance	0.013	0.005	0.018	1.783	0.023

Source: Morgan Guaranty.

comes in first when judged by mean absolute value.[27] Switzerland comes in fourth, and France comes in last, by all measures.

Not much can be made of this specific ordering. Differentials of much less than half a percent are probably not worth worrying about for present purposes. By that criterion, Japan, the United Kingdom, Germany, Switzerland, Canada, and the United States all currently have open capital markets. Of the largest Western countries, only France belongs in a fundamentally different category. The typical differential between the Euro-franc rate and domestic French interest rates is 10 times as large as that for the other countries. Deviations as large as 25 percent occur. French capital controls discourage capital from flowing out of the country into the world market where higher returns are available.[28] Most of the smaller industrial countries,

---

27. Judged by the variance of the differential, Japan comes in second during the recent period. The variance is probably a better measure of the extent to which domestic interest rates are tied to world rates, because it allows for a constant term that could be due, for example in the case of the US dollar, to the existence of reserve requirements in domestic banking and their absence in the Eurocurrency market.

28. Capital controls, in effect in France since 1968, were tightened when the Socialist government came to power in May 1981. The very large French interest differentials (for example, 25.5 percent on March 18, 1983) occur when imminent devaluation of the franc is expected. Some implications of French capital controls are discussed in Frankel (1982a).

and all less developed countries with a few exceptions like Hong Kong, also have capital controls.

The graph and statistics on the gensaki interest rate are a useful illustration of the liberalization that took place after 1979. But the gensaki market is only one market. Murchison and Solomon (p. 62) argue that it is a small market and identify many other specific areas where Japanese authorities are argued to discourage, explicitly or implicitly, net capital inflow so as to bias the value of the yen downward.

A result from economic theory should be noted here. If it is conceded that foreigners are entirely free to acquire gensaki, then the proposition that they are not entirely free to acquire some other Japanese security, or that the gensaki market is small, would not be sufficient in itself to imply an effect on the exchange rate. If there were excess demand for yen assets, eager foreigners would bid down the rate of return paid on assets like gensaki that they are able to hold. Japanese residents would respond to the lower rate of return by moving into the other assets; the aggregate demand for yen need not change. To obtain a downward effect on the value of the yen, it would have to be argued that foreigners are excluded from holding important Japanese securities *and* that those securities are poor substitutes for the securities that foreigners can hold. Although gensaki are probably poor substitutes for other Japanese assets in many respects, they are obviously the same with respect to currency of denomination.

Thus a claim that the existence of controls on capital inflow, or the existence of a restricted menu of assets, can enforce a condition of unsatisfied market demand for a currency is a very strong claim. OECD (1984a, p. 63) concludes:

It is admittedly true that the range of financial assets available to foreign investors is narrower (and transactions costs higher) than in the United States. But the market is not so narrow as to frustrate the foreign desire to hold yen in one form or another. Even prior to 1979—when foreign access to Tokyo was much more limited—market expectations of a yen appreciation were on occasion translated in massive capital inflows that pushed the [value of the yen] up. . . .

The same could be said of Germany and Switzerland in the 1960s and early 1970s: an array of capital controls far more formidable than Japan has today did not succeed in keeping foreign capital from flowing in and the currencies from appreciating. Especially with net capital outflows from Japan since 1981, it is hard to see how natural market pressures, even if frustrated by remaining distortions, could currently be working to push up the yen.

We turn now to a consideration of those specific measures involved in the 1983–84 liberalization that relate to international flows. As in the other categories of measures considered in later sections, the discussion of institutional detail will seem tedious to some—the casual American reader—and will seem superficial to others—most Japanese readers. The level of the presentation is intended to benefit readers who are interested in the subject but unfamiliar with the details. Any other readers are invited to concentrate on the analysis at the beginning of each subsection and skip the paragraphs dealing with specific measures. It should also be noted that the classification into four categories is necessarily somewhat arbitrary; some of the measures listed in one section also have effects that belong in another section.

New Measures to Liberalize Capital Outflows

We begin with the liberalization of restrictions on the outflow of capital from Japan. As we have seen, these restrictions were partly liberalized in 1980, with the subsequent result of a net capital outflow and depreciation of the yen, but were not eliminated completely in 1981–83 in an effort to limit the yen's depreciation.[29] The further liberalization of controls on capital outflow can be expected to weaken the yen.[30]

American businessmen sometimes complain that they are not sufficiently free to borrow in Japan. Often they do not recognize that this complaint is inconsistent with the complaint that the Japanese authorities keep the yen artificially undervalued. Again, greater capital flows from Japan to the United States would weaken the yen against the dollar, not strengthen it.[31] Those who do recognize the point divide on their policy prescriptions. Bergsten (1982, p. 1071; 1984, pp. 4, 27–29) argues that the goal of raising the value

---

29. GAO (1984, pp. 21, 41); Freeman (1984, p. 15); and Hama (1983, p. 7).

30. Niskanen (1983) agrees that removal of all Japanese capital controls that remained after 1980 would most likely lead to increased capital outflow and a weakening of the yen, as do Solomon (1983, p. 93) and Kanemitsu (1983, p. 317). On the other hand, it should be acknowledged that, especially in traditionally weak-currency countries, the danger that investors will not be able to get their money out again can work to discourage net capital inflow.

31. Of course if an American borrows in yen, *and holds the proceeds in yen,* then there would be no effect on the exchange rate, because the change in American assets cancels out the change in liabilities. But holding the proceeds in yen counts as a separate transaction, a credit in the Japanese capital account. "Borrowing abroad" normally means that the proceeds are converted into dollars.

of the yen against the dollar, and thus alleviating both the trade imbalance and the resultant protectionist pressures, is urgent enough that it justifies encouraging the Japanese to maintain, and even increase, whatever controls on outflow they now have.

Lee Morgan, on the other hand, believes that the longer term goal of liberalizing all capital flows warrants encouraging the Japanese to continue even those liberalization measures that immediately increase outflows and weaken the yen. Under Secretary Sprinkel (1983, p. 4) agrees:

Removal of controls of all kinds on the Japanese capital market will help promote increased internationalization of the yen and will result in greater access by foreigners to Japanese capital. To pressure the Japanese to pursue "stop-go" policies in this area would simply frustrate the longer-term goal of liberalization and would increase market uncertainty about freedom of access to Japan's capital markets.

Secretary Regan, at least in the initial stages of the exercise, often appeared to miss altogether the point that allowing more capital outflow from Japan would weaken the yen. A November 10 *Washington Post* story reported on a Metromedia interview with the secretary:

Regan also said that Japan should open up its capital markets so that the US companies could borrow money there. "They won't share [their] savings with anyone else. Any Japanese company can come over here to the United States and borrow in our markets and take our savings; we cannot go over to their markets with impunity and borrow whatever we want over there, so what we're saying is, open up your capital markets and learn to share. *And in that way you will help to strengthen your yen and our dollar won't be nearly as strong.*" [Emphasis added.]

Whatever the merits of the 1983–84 US push for liberalization of Japanese capital markets, one would feel better about it if it had firmer foundations in economic reasoning.

Four measures to liberalize restrictions on capital outflow were part of the US campaign launched in October 1983.

SAMURAI BONDS

Since the early 1970s, nonresidents have been able to borrow in Japan by issuing yen-denominated samurai bonds (Eken, p. 12; Pigott, p. 39). But as

Murchison and Solomon point out, there were restrictions on which foreign institutions were allowed to participate,[32] and on the total amount of yen-denominated bonds that they could issue per quarter.[33] In a move that *Euromoney* (24 June 1984, p. 29) asserted "might have the largest nominal impact of any of the regulatory changes," the Japanese securities industry recently agreed with the Ministry of Finance on relaxation of many of the restrictions:[34] relaxing the credit rating required for issues, reducing the waiting period between issues, and raising the permitted size of each issue.

"ADMINISTRATIVE GUIDANCE" RESTRICTING OVERSEAS LENDING BY JAPANESE BANKS

As Murchison and Solomon (p. 55) point out, "controls of capital flows do not always take the form of written laws or regulations." In particular, the Ministry of Finance in 1982 and 1983 put quantitative limits or quotas on overseas yen lending by Japanese banks, in part due to "prudential" concerns (for example, those relating to the international debt problem), in part to support the value of the yen.[35] Effective April 1984, the Ministry of Finance relaxed its guidelines.[36] The May 1984 report of the Yen/Dollar Working Group (p. 18) officially recognized that nonprudential limits on overseas yen lending from Japanese banks had been abolished.

SALES IN JAPAN OF FOREIGN COMMERCIAL PAPER AND CDs

Plans in 1982, to allow Japanese banks and securities companies to trade in foreign-issued commercial paper and certificates of deposit, had been suspended, largely to avoid the downward effect of capital outflow on the yen. As part of the liberalization package, the Ministry of Finance allowed such trading, effective April 1, 1984.[37]

---

32. Murchison and Solomon (1983, pp. 69–70) and *Euromoney,* 24 June 1984, p. 25. Initially the main issuers were international agencies, according to Pigott (1983, pp. 39, 43); Sakakibara and Kondoh (1984); and OECD (1984, pp. 58–67). World Bank issues predominate in a secondary market.

33. Murchison and Solomon (1983, pp. 70–71); GAO (1984, p. 48).

34. Freeman (1984, pp. 8, A10); OECD (1984, p. 80).

35. GAO (1984, p. 21), cites the IMF *Annual Report on Exchange Restrictions.* Other references are Hama (1983, p. 7); Freeman (1984, p. 8); and Murchison and Solomon (1983, pp. 72–73).

36. Freeman (1984, p. A10); *World Financial Markets* (June 1984), p. 9.

37. Freeman (1984, p. A6); OECD (1984, p. 80); Sakakibara and Kondoh (1984, pp. xxi, 48).

DEPOSITS OF RESIDENTS IN OVERSEAS FINANCIAL INSTITUTIONS

According to the May 1984 report (pp. 18–19), the Yen/Dollar Working Group discussed the subject of foreign bank accounts. It concluded that Japanese residents are not authorized to hold overseas accounts for investment purposes, but are authorized to hold such accounts for overseas business activities. (Since December 1980 Japanese residents have been free to hold foreign-currency accounts with domestic banks, even for investment purposes, which is not the case for US residents.[38])

New Measures to Liberalize Capital Inflows

We now turn from Japanese measures that liberalize capital outflows, to those that liberalize capital inflows. These measures are of course the ones that could be expected to have a non-negative effect on the value of the yen, but they are few in number. As of 1983 nonresidents were already free to acquire all types of Japanese securities except for equity investments in certain areas (GAO, p. 49).

"DESIGNATED COMPANY" SYSTEM FOR DIRECT INVESTMENT

The 1980 Foreign Exchange and Trade Control Law abolished the requirement that foreigners obtain government approval for each direct investment, as well as each portfolio investment. But, as Murchison and Solomon (pp. 82–86) and other Americans complained, in 1983 foreign direct investment was still restricted under the "designated company" system. In 11 designated companies, foreigners were restricted from acquiring more than specified percentages (ranging from 25 percent, for a silk spinning company, to 50 percent for a number of petroleum companies). In response to US pressure, the Ministry of Finance agreed to seek elimination of the designated company system as part of an omnibus bill written in October 1983. The elimination appears as one of the eight measures in the November 10, 1983, Regan-Takeshita agreement. The bill was introduced in the Diet on March 27, 1984, and passed on May 18.

---

38. Sakakibara and Kondoh (1984, pp. xxi, 17); International Monetary Fund (1983, p. 283).

REAL ESTATE

Another complaint was that foreigners wishing to acquire real estate in Japan were subject to a screening requirement under the 1980 law. In practice such investment had been permitted automatically, except perhaps for "highly speculative" acquisitions. As part of the same omnibus bill written in October 1983, the Japanese government eliminated the screening requirement. But there does not seem to have been any excess demand for Japanese property. Freeman (p. 16) believes, "New direct investment in real estate or in the eleven previously proscribed Japanese industries is not likely to be extensive."

Direct Measures for Japanese Government Borrowing in the United States

Although the US side rejected the idea (for example, Bergsten 1984) of encouraging Japan to raise barriers to capital outflow, it did adopt the proposal of Bergsten, Morgan, Murchison-Solomon, and others to press the Japanese government to do some of its own borrowing in the United States. This proposal could be viewed as a form of artificial government intervention in the capital markets, in that it is clear that the agencies involved would not otherwise choose to borrow at 13 percent in New York when they could borrow at 7 percent in Tokyo. The interest differential can be attributed to market expectations of future depreciation of the dollar against the yen (at 6 percent a year, as in table 1), which would work to reduce Japanese borrowing costs; but government agencies are often wary of appearing to speculate in foreign exchange.

"NAKASONE BONDS"

Financing the Japanese government deficit overseas instead of in Japan, that is, the proposed issue of "Nakasone bonds," is one of the measures on the Murchison-Solomon list. As of 1983, the government itself was not able to borrow overseas under Japanese law. In response to US pressure, the Japanese cabinet in February 1984 approved for submission to the Diet legislation, which was subsequently passed, to enable such overseas bond issues in the future. However, in 1984 the government appeared to have no plans to use the new borrowing authority.

ISSUE IN NEW YORK OF GOVERNMENT AGENCY BONDS

As of 1983, government-affiliated agencies were already able to borrow overseas and had done so in the past. To alleviate temporarily US pressure in this area, the Japanese Development Bank issued $100 million of government-guaranteed seven-year notes in New York on February 29, 1984. The Japanese swapped the dollar proceeds for a Swiss franc security, thereby reducing the interest cost to 6 percent; Switzerland has been Japan's preferred source of overseas financing in the recent past. The swap should have negated the upward effect on the yen of the New York issue, if it is the case that the issuer of the Swiss franc security would otherwise have borrowed in dollars, but such an effect would in any case have been minuscule.

The Japanese budget of Fiscal Year 1984 authorizes a large increase in overseas issue of government-guaranteed bonds. But it would probably take renewed US pressure before the Japanese government or affiliated agencies would undertake further issues in New York. And the US Treasury is beginning to realize that it is becoming increasingly dependent on the net inflow of foreign capital to the United States to hold down its own rising borrowing costs. In fall 1984, the Treasury created a new variety of US government bonds to be sold to foreigners, and a high-level delegation visited Tokyo and other capitals to explain their attractive features to investors. There are some signs that political forces may now start operating in the direction of pressuring the Japanese to buy securities in the United States rather then to sell them.

It would take a truly flexible intellect to deny in the abstract any link between budget deficits and interest rates, and at the same time have second thoughts in practice about encouraging competition from foreign governments for funds in New York. But as it becomes increasingly difficult to finance the US deficit, it would seem to become increasingly unlikely that the Treasury will push the Japanese government for further bond issues in the United States, the yen/dollar issue not withstanding.

4   Internationalization of the Yen

The US–Japanese Yen/Dollar Working Group came into more direct conflict over measures in the second category, internationalization of the yen, than over those in any of the other three categories. The US side pointed out that the yen is not as prominent in world financial markets as the Japanese economy is in world goods markets. (Japan surpassed West Germany in economic size in the late 1960s and is now about one-third the size of the United States.) Obviously, if central banks, multinational corporations, and other investors around the world significantly increased their demand for yen, it would have a positive effect on the value of the yen. On the other hand, an observed increase in use of the yen would not imply an increase in its value if the change were the result of a rise in supply as much as of a rise in demand.

The question of controversy is the extent to which demand for yen is currently less than it would otherwise be due to factors under the control of the Japanese government. Three or four of the topics on Lee Morgan's wish list are identified with internationalization of the yen. (See the excerpts from the Murchison-Solomon Executive Summary in appendix B.) The November Regan-Takeshita announcement also included four such measures. One item on both lists—easing guidelines on the issue of yen bonds in the Euromarket, for example, by Japanese corporations—proved to be an area of contention in the subsequent Yen/Dollar Working Group meetings.

The General Issue of "Internationalization"

The US side took the line that, now that Japan is the second largest trading nation in the world after the United States, it is time for the Japanese currency to take a role commensurate with that status.[39]

It is inherently difficult to judge what is the relevant standard of laissez-faire or market equilibrium in the use of a currency. Even assuming the Japanese government wanted to prevent exporters around the world from invoicing in yen, borrowers from issuing bonds denominated in yen, and central banks from acquiring yen reserves, one could argue that there is

---

39. In Tokyo on March 24 Regan told a Japanese audience: "If Japan is No. 2, Japan should try harder in order to become more like what the rest of the world is doing" (appendix C). It would perhaps have been more gracious for the US side to suggest a cooperative enterprise of overseeing the natural evolution of the yen into a key international currency, than to lecture a sovereign allied country, one with a highly successful economy, that there is something wrong with its financial markets.

nothing it could do to stop them. On the other hand, the choice of vehicle currency is to an extent endogenous. Incremental steps by the Japanese government to make it more convenient for foreigners to hold yen might have a noticeable effect.

There are large economies of scale in the choice of vehicle currency: to save transaction costs, an exporter, borrower, or investor will use any currency already used by the economic actors with whom he generally deals (importers, lenders, and issuers, in the three respective cases, and banks in each case). As McKinnon (1979) and Krugman (1984), among others, point out, an implication of this line of argument is that it is most efficient for the world economy to have a single vehicle currency. That currency since World War II has, of course, been the dollar. The McKinnon-Krugman argument would suggest that promoting the yen as a vehicle currency would be counterproductive until such time as we expect it to supplant the dollar.

There are counterarguments, to the effect that the world monetary system would be more stable if it rested more evenly on several currencies as against the current heavy reliance on the dollar. There is the old argument that the "dollar overhang," in reserve holdings outside the United States, represents a source of potential instability. This argument has not been heard much since the end of the 1970s, when the risks of accelerated dollar depreciation were much on observers' minds. But it in large part gave rise to the creation of the special drawing right (SDR) and the European currency unit (ECU), which are still being promoted by their creators (the International Monetary Fund and the European Community, respectively). Indeed the use of both units, by borrowers to denominate loans, by central banks to peg their exchange rate, and so forth, is gradually increasing over time. Clearly many countries of Latin America would not have accumulated so much indebtedness in 1980–84 if their currencies had been pegged to the SDR rather than the dollar, and would not now be finding their debt so onerous to service if more of it had been denominated in currencies other than the dollar. As a natural— but perhaps belated—reaction, recent debt-rescheduling arrangements, for Mexico in particular, have allowed for increased use of the yen and other nondollar currencies in denominating the loans.

It is true that Japanese government policy with regard to the international use of the yen was in the 1970s on the discouraging side of neutral. The same could be said of German policy with regard to the mark and Swiss policy with regard to the franc. The Japanese monetary authorities, like the German and Swiss, were concerned that extensive foreign holdings of their currency would reduce their degree of control over the money supply, and would increase the variability of the exchange rate. But it can be argued that capital flows do not affect a country's monetary base unless the central bank intervenes in the foreign exchange market, and that the question of exchange rate variability depends on the sources of disturbances and the values of parameters.[40] In the past, the fact that the yen has been less widely used internationally than the mark or the dollar has not prevented the yen from undergoing larger swings in exchange value than the mark or dollar.

Whatever the inclinations of the Japanese authorities, use of the yen has increased rapidly over the last 10 years, relative to the low levels of the past, as is documented below. In particular, international demand for the yen as an investment currency has increased, in response to Japan's low and stable inflation rate and the consequent favorable rate of return on yen relative to other currencies.

Before turning to the specific measures to internationalize the yen that have figured in the events of the last year, it is worth taking note that the official policy of the Japanese government, at least the Ministry of Finance, has shifted to the encouraging side of neutral. A public commitment to the principle of internationalization appeared first in the Regan-Takeshita announcement of November 1983. The May report of the Yen/Dollar Working Group (p. 25) agreed that "it is fitting for the yen to play a role in international financial transactions that reflects Japan's importance as a great trading and financial world power."

Use of the Yen as a Reserve Currency

No fewer than 4 of the 11 items on the Murchison-Solomon list urge a shift toward increased holding of yen reserves by monetary authorities in the United States, West Germany, Saudi Arabia, and other countries (and a shift by the Japanese authorities toward decreased holding of dollar reserves). Such portfolio shifts most often take place in the form of foreign exchange intervention. Admittedly, governments can add to their holdings of particular currencies in some ways that do not qualify as foreign exchange intervention narrowly defined. For example, the Bank of Japan, like other central banks, receives dollars as interest payments on its previously acquired dollar holdings.

---

40. The two arguments are made by Sakakibara and Kondoh (1984, pp. 104–6) and Freeman (1984, appendix D), respectively.

More importantly, third-country central banks can shift their portfolios from dollars to yen without intervening in the market for their own currencies.[41] But, as we saw in section 2, the Japanese authorities have since 1980 shown more enthusiasm for operations in the foreign exchange markets to reduce the yen/dollar rate than have the US authorities. Nor is the US reluctance to intervene clearly misplaced. Most American economists agree with the report of the Versailles summit intervention working group (released in April 1983), that foreign exchange intervention is unlikely to be effective if it is sterilized so that the money supply is unchanged. Many economists also agree with the "Feldstein doctrine" that the main problem lies with the monetary-fiscal mix in the United States, and that if one takes the growing budget deficits as given, there are good arguments why the value of the dollar should be high.[42]

Table 5 presents the figures for the foreign exchange reserve holdings of the world's central banks, expressed as shares allocated to dollars, marks, yen, pounds, Swiss francs, French francs, and guilders. Alone among the seven currencies, the yen share has more than doubled in the last eight years. It ranks third; holdings of yen (mostly by OPEC and Asian countries) are greater than the combined holdings of pounds and French francs, two currencies to which many nations in Africa and Asia have in the past been pegged. The yen share does look small compared to the dollar and mark. This is the basis of the Treasury position that Japan's currency has a long way to go before attaining "No. 2" status.

The question remains what the Japanese government could do to encourage foreign central banks to hold more yen. Some of the 1984 measures discussed below, such as the removal of restrictions on the Euro-yen market and the further development of a short-term market in government securities in Japan,

---

41. Bergsten and Williamson (forthcoming 1985) analyze shifts of reserve holdings by central banks. They argue that such shifts, for example into the mark in the 1970s and back out of the mark in the 1980s, have worked to exaggerate exchange rate swings. This argument would tend to cast some doubt on the desirability of increased central bank holdings of yen.

42. The argument begins with the standard proposition that the budget deficit pushes up real interest rates and crowds out investment. Given that it does, a capital inflow that appreciates the dollar has the advantage of mitigating the rise in real interest rates. Attempts to bring the value of the dollar down by sterilized foreign exchange intervention would increase the supply of Treasury securities in the marketplace. Attempts to do so by imposing capital controls would shut off foreign purchases of US securities. Either way, the interest rate would rise. The argument is made in the Council of Economic Advisers' 1983 and 1984 reports and by Feldstein (1984). The term "Feldstein doctrine" has been used by Williamson (1983, p. 32).

TABLE 5   **Share of national currencies in total identified official holdings of foreign exchange, end of years, 1976–83** (percentages)

	1976	1977	1978	1979	1980	1981	1982	1983
US dollar	76.5	77.9	75.6	72.8	66.7	69.4	68.5	69.1
Deutsche mark	9.0	9.2	11.0	12.6	15.1	13.2	12.5	11.9
Japanese yen	2.0	2.3	3.2	3.5	4.2	4.1	4.2	4.2
Pound sterling	1.8	1.7	1.7	2.0	3.0	2.2	2.5	2.6
Swiss franc	2.3	2.4	2.3	2.7	3.2	2.8	2.7	2.4
French franc	1.6	1.3	1.2	1.4	1.7	1.4	1.4	1.2
Netherlands guilder	0.9	0.9	0.9	1.1	1.3	1.2	1.0	0.8
Unspecified	5.9	4.3	4.2	4.0	4.8	5.7	7.2	7.8

Note: Starting with 1974, the value of ECUs issued against US dollars is added to the value of US dollars, but the value of ECUs issued against gold is excluded from the total distributed here.
Source: IMF *Annual Report 1984*, table 12.

may make it easier for central banks and other nonresidents to hold interest-earning yen assets. Freeman (p. 14) suggests that the Japanese government's shift toward official encouragement of international use of the yen as a reserve currency began earlier:

Starting in about 1980, the Japanese authorities actively supported official diversification into yen-denominated assets by several means including freeing the interest rate on official yen deposits in Japan and encouraging purchases—particularly by OPEC authorities—of yen-denominated assets.

Use of Yen for Denominating and Financing Trade

Murchison and Solomon point out that a relatively small share of Japanese trade is invoiced or financed in yen as opposed to dollars. Table 6 shows that the share of Japanese exports denominated in yen has increased as rapidly as the share of central bank reserve holdings. But as Murchison and Solomon (pp. 88, 102–3) emphasize, the share of Japanese imports denominated in yen is still very small. They argue that this depresses the transaction demand for yen, and thereby depresses its value.

Murchison and Solomon (p. 88) carry the argument rather far in claiming that, "In the case of West Germany and other developed countries, let alone the United States, all or most of exports and imports are denominated and

TABLE 6 **Percentage of Japanese trade invoiced in yen**

	EXPORTS	IMPORTS		
	Source: MITI Trade Bureau, July 1984	*Source: Eken (forthcoming, p. 28)*		
1984				
June	38.6	About 3.0		
May	39.6			
Apr.	39.1			
Mar.	39.4			
Feb.	38.6			
1983		*Source: OECD (1984, p. 62)*		
Jan.	38.6			
Dec.	39.2	34.5		3.0
Nov.	38.8			
Oct.	38.1			
		Source: Ministry of Finance, as reported by Hama (1983, p. 81)		
1983	39.3			
1982	38.1	38.2		
1981	34.8	31.9		
1980	28.9	28.9	2.4	2.4
1979	24.9	24.8	2.4	2.4
1978	19.8	24.8		1.6
1977	18.8			1.2
1976	19.4	17.0	0.9	
1975	17.0	0.9	0.3	
1970				

financed in their currencies.'' This statement seems to ignore the fact that if a German exporter denominates the payment he receives in marks, the importer must necessarily pay in marks. Unless the developed countries trade more with the Third World than with each other, which is not the case, they cannot possibly denominate their exports *and* their imports in their own currencies.

The argument that Japanese importers are to be blamed for paying in dollars rather than yen was carried even farther by Secretary Regan in remarks to the Keidanren in Tokyo on March 24, 1984.[43] Most commonly in manufactures trade among the European countries, the exporter invoices in his own currency (except when exporting to the United States, in which case the dollar is often used). As a consequence the importer cannot make payment in his own currency. The GAO report found that 82 percent of German exports are denominated in marks, but only 36 percent to 43 percent of imports (into Germany, the United Kingdom, and France) are denominated in local currencies.[44]

The Japanese numbers shown in table 6 are admittedly very low, especially in the case of imports. Eken (1984, p. 28) gives four reasons why such a low share of Japanese trade is invoiced in yen:

- An unusually high fraction of Japanese imports is not manufactured goods, but oil, agricultural products, and other raw materials, all of which are normally invoiced in dollars worldwide.[45]

- In the past, quantitative controls on bank lending may have encouraged importers to obtain trade credit abroad rather than in Japan.

- In the more distant past, in the case of Japanese exports to countries outside Europe, lack of forward yen markets outside Europe has made it more difficult for foreign importers to hedge exchange risk if the export is invoiced in yen.

- Due to the absence of a market in banker's acceptances in Japan, traders depend on the dollar banker's acceptance market in New York.[46]

---

43. See paragraph 3, appendix C. Secretary Regan appears to advance the novel theory that importers, rather than *making* payment when they buy goods, *receive* payment. It is easy enough for anyone in oral remarks to mix up inflows and outflows or exports and imports. Unfortunately, the Secretary repeated the same point, in very similar language, in a press conference later the same day. The two possible explanations are: he meant exports instead of imports; and by "ask for in way of payment" he meant "ask to be allowed to make payment in."

44. Krugman (1984, p. 270), Eken (forthcoming, p. 28), and Sakakibara and Kondoh (1984, table 4–2–3), give similar figures. The figures for the United States are 98 percent for exports and 85 percent for imports GAO (1984, p. 25). However, OECD (1984, p. 62) gives somewhat lower numbers for percentage of exports invoiced in domestic currency: "over 60 percent" for major European countries and "about 90 percent" for the United States.

45. Freeman (1984, p. 19), (GAO, 1984, p. 24), Hama (1983, p. 81), *World Financial Markets* (June 1984), p. 8, Sakakibara and Kondoh (1984, pp. xxvii, 70), and OECD (1984, p. 62) make the same point. The GAO puts fuels and raw materials at two-thirds of imports. In 1983, SITC categories 0 to 4 constituted 74 percent of imports classified by commodity (OECD 1984a, p. 91).

46. *World Financial Markets* (June 1984), p. 8, GAO (1984, p. 24), Sakakibara and Kondoh (1984, pp. xiv, 28), and OECD (1984, p. 62) as well point to the fact that import financing in yen is not fully developed, and in particular to the absence of banker's acceptances.

A fifth reason is that a higher fraction of Japan's trade than of Europe's trade is with the Western Hemisphere; more than half of Japanese exports to Western Europe are in fact denominated in yen.[47] A possible sixth reason is that Americans find it more convenient to think in terms of dollars than yen and that Japanese businessmen, as they do in most aspects of marketing, accommodate themselves to foreign customers' currency preferences better than do American businessmen.

One of the 11 measures on the Murchison-Solomon list is "a substantial increase in the percentage" of Japanese exports and imports that are denominated and financed in yen. Murchison and Solomon do not state precisely what measures the Japanese government should take to bring about this change in the habits of Japanese exporters (let alone foreign exporters to Japan). But each of the three measures discussed in the remainder of this subsection is considered to be relevant.

"REAL DEMAND" RULE FOR FORWARD EXCHANGE MARKET

In the past, forward exchange transactions within Japan were restricted to those that covered specific "bona fide" transactions, as when an exporter wants to sell anticipated dollar proceeds forward. This has tended to retard development of the forward exchange market in Tokyo. In the November Regan-Takeshita announcement, the Ministry of Finance agreed to eliminate this restriction, known as the real demand rule. The change became effective April 1, 1984, as acknowledged in the May report of the Yen/Dollar Working Group.

BANKER'S ACCEPTANCES

A banker's acceptance market is a market on which a bank, having provided international trade financing to a customer, can resell the claim against the customer to others under its guarantee. No such market exists in Japan. In the November Regan-Takeshita announcement, the Japanese agreed to expedite an ongoing study concerning establishment of a yen-denominated banker's acceptance market. In the May report of the Yen/Dollar Working Group (p. 17), the Ministry of Finance agreed that the creation of such a

---

47. Sakakibara and Kondoh (1984, table 4–2–1); OECD (1984, n. 53).

market would be instrumental to the internationalization of the yen, and set a deadline of the end of 1984 for establishing a concrete scheme, with the market to become operative shortly thereafter. In October the Federation of Bankers' Associations of Japan proposed specific terms for a market in banker's acceptances to be established in April 1985.[48]

It is important to note that when a bank lends to an importer in yen rather than dollars, there is no effect on the *net* supply of yen assets to the private sector. Furthermore, as Freeman (p. 19) points out, either party is free to reverse its yen position on the foreign exchange market. Thus a shift from dollar to yen financing does not necessarily have a positive effect on the value of the yen. The Treasury argues that, as the use of the yen in trade and finance (essentially as a unit of account) increases over time, the demand for yen (as an asset) will also increase.

PREFERENTIAL IMPORT FINANCING BY THE BANK OF JAPAN

In November 1983 the Bank of Japan reactivated a program under which, through banks, it provides yen trade credit on preferential terms to importers who would otherwise borrow dollars abroad. Since the alternative is for the importer to borrow abroad, this measure would seem to raise the net capital outflow from Japan and thus weaken the yen. It is possible that this measure was never intended as a response to the US yen/dollar campaign.

Use of the Yen in the Euromarket

Japanese restrictions on the Euro-yen bond market were the area of greatest contention between the US and Japanese sides in the Yen/Dollar Working Group.[49] As late as early May, the Euro-yen subject was enough of a sticking point to jeopardize the spring deadline set by Regan and Takeshita for agreement. The disagreements were soon resolved, but the subsequent May 29 report (p. 25) acknowledged that there had been "some difference of views between Japan and the United States on the role of the Euromarket in internationalizing the yen."

---

48. *Nihon Keizai Shimbun*, 23 October 1984, p. 3.
49. Interview with Oba in the *Japan Economic Journal* (3 July 1984).

At first glance, the Euromarket may seem a surprising area for contention. The Euromarkets originally developed, in London and elsewhere, precisely in order to be free of regulation by the country in whose currency the issues are denominated. How can the Japanese government prevent a corporation from issuing a yen bond in London?

The most important category of borrower interested in Euro-yen issues consists of corporations that reside in Japan, and thus are subject to Japanese restrictions. But even nonresident corporations are in practice bound. There is an international understanding that each country's banks and securities companies will take the role of lead-manager on a Eurobond issue denominated in its own currency, which in practice places the issues under the jurisdiction of the bank's home-country government. For example, mark-denominated bonds, wherever issued, are known to be subject to review by the German government. A bank that violated the international understanding might face retaliation in the future should it seek to do business in the home country of the currency in question.

EURO-YEN BOND ISSUES BY NONRESIDENTS

Effective December 1, 1984, the Ministry of Finance allowed non-Japanese corporations, and other institutions, to issue yen bonds in the Euromarket under the same rules as they are allowed to issue samurai bonds in Japan. It also made a commitment, in the May report of the Yen/Dollar Working Group (p. 27), to liberalize the credit rating required for issuers, effective April 1, 1985. No restrictions will be imposed on the size and number of Euro-yen bond issues by nonresidents.

EURO-YEN BOND ISSUES BY RESIDENTS

Murchison and Solomon (p. 110) urge that the Japanese government eliminate all restrictions on Eurobond issues by residents. As agreed in the Regan-Takeshita announcement of November, the Ministry of Finance eased guidelines on the issue of Euro-yen bonds by Japanese residents, effective April 1, 1984. For the first time, it allowed many corporations already able to issue yen bonds in Japan also to issue them in the Euromarket, and simultaneously relaxed the net asset requirements that the corporations must meet for either kind of issue. As a result, 30 Japanese corporations now qualify for straight issues and 108 for convertible issues (OECD, 1984a, p. 80). No restrictions exist on what banks or securities firms can take the lead-manager role in any Eurobond issue. However, to insulate the domestic bond market, Euro-yen bonds cannot be resold to Japanese residents within the first 180 days after issuance.[50]

Some observers believe that the Euromarket liberalization potentially will have the greatest impact of all the measures on the structure of Japanese capital markets, if not on the yen/dollar exchange rate.[51] However, most seem to agree with the Treasury that the demand for Eurobonds issued by Japanese corporations will be limited if the government continues to withhold taxes on interest payments to foreigners. Indeed, in the six months after the removal of restrictions, no such Eurobonds were issued.[52]

WITHHOLDING TAX ON EARNINGS FROM EUROBONDS ISSUED BY RESIDENTS

The Japanese government withholds taxes from earnings on most securities issued by Japanese residents, whether held by residents or nonresidents. The withholding tax rate that a nonresident must pay on interest from Japanese securities (20 percent, unless reduced by bilateral treaty as it has been, to 10 percent, with the United States) is higher than it is on some countries' securities. For example, the United States has for some time had tax treaties with Germany and the United Kingdom that reduce the withholding rate on each others' earnings to zero. Because Japanese withholding reduces the attractiveness of Japanese securities for nonresidents, it acts to reduce capital inflow to Japan and to weaken the yen. For this reason, Murchison and Solomon (p. 109) urge that the withholding tax for nonresidents be rescinded.

The tax subject came up in the context of Euro-yen bonds. In the November Regan-Takeshita announcement, the Ministry of Finance agreed that the tax would be "reviewed, having due regard to maintaining proper taxation including the withholding tax system." However, this review by the Japanese

---

50. Report of the Yen/Dollar Working Group (1984, pp. 27–28); Sakakibara and Kondoh (1984, pp. xx, 45–46).
51. Hamada (1984, p. 13) and Freeman (1984, pp. 16–18). In his appendix C, Freeman argues that the effect on the exchange rate of relaxing the Euro-yen borrowing constraint is ambiguous.
52. *Nihon Keizai Shimbun*, 31 July 1984.

tax bureau subsequently came out unfavorable to removal, on the grounds that current Japanese practice treats resident and nonresident investors symmetrically. A 1982 effort in the United States to extend US withholding to all domestic securities had been defeated in the Congress. As a result, as of May 1984 it was the United States, not Japan, that discriminated against nonresident investors with respect to withholding. (What constitutes symmetric treatment is often ambiguous when tax systems differ across countries.)

As the US side pointed out in the Yen/Dollar Working Group, the US government was in the process of eliminating its withholding tax on earnings paid to nonresidents. This change, which became effective July 18, 1984, has the disadvantage, under current conditions, that it further encourages capital to flow to the United States and thus puts upward pressure on the dollar. As a competitor in the world market for funds, Japan would now have to reduce its withholding tax just to stay even with US policy.

The Japanese side expressed no willingness to consider the elimination of its withholding tax system within the domestic market (p. 14). It did agree to expedite its study of withholding on interest paid to nonresidents, with a report by the end of 1984 and legislation, if any, submitted to the Diet at the subsequent session. Since the US elimination of tax withholding on earnings paid to nonresidents, Germany and France have taken steps in the same direction. It may be inevitable that Japan will have to remove its own withholding on interest paid to nonresidents in order to compete for funds in world capital markets.

PARTICIPATION OF BANKS IN THE EURO-YEN MARKET

In the May report of the Yen/Dollar Working Group (p. 30), the Ministry of Finance agreed by the end of the year to allow foreign and Japanese banks to issue and trade short-term negotiable Euro-yen CDs outside of Japan. It also liberalized Euro-yen lending by banking syndicates. Banks can now lend Euro-yen with maturities of one year or less to Japanese residents, rather than just to nonresidents.

OFFSHORE BANKING FACILITY IN TOKYO

An offshore, or international, banking facility (IBF) is one where banks can accept deposits from nonresidents, without having to meet reserve requirements and other restrictions of the country in which the facility is physically located. The United States established such a facility in New York in 1981. Since then, some Japanese have argued that the same should be done in Tokyo, although the government's initial reaction was negative.[53]

Murchison and Solomon (pp. 110–11) urge that Japan establish an IBF. This proposed measure could be classed in the category of section 3: it would help grease the wheels of capital movement. As such, under current conditions it would have the same negative effect on the value of the yen as some of the other measures considered above. More capital would flow out than in, because Japan has an excess of national savings over investment, as reflected in its low real interest rate, relative to the United States. The topic of a proposed offshore banking facility has been chosen to close this section because an IBF is essentially a member unit of the world Euromarket, and because the US side's argument in favor of it was that it would help promote the internationalization of the yen. It remains to be seen whether such a facility is to be established.

5   Treatment of US Financial Institutions in Japan

The US yen/dollar campaign quickly gathered momentum, among other reasons, because a number of its measures were in the interest of US banks and other financial institutions. This category of measures is best viewed as opening Japan to the export of banking services from the United States, and thus kept conceptually distinct from measures promoting the export or import of capital per se. (This is not to deny that some of the specific measures discussed below have effects of both kinds.) As such they must be recognized as another force tending to depreciate the yen against the dollar, rather than to appreciate it. This is so because Japanese imports of banking services— like Japanese imports of computer software, beef, citrus, or anything else—

---

53. Pigott (1983, p. 41); Freeman (1984, pp. A9–A10); Sakakibara and Kondoh (1984, pp. xv– xvi, 32–35).

reduce Japan's balance of payments surplus in goods and services, and thereby reduce the demand for yen.

However, the positive effects of such a depreciation of the yen on the Japanese trade surplus, which is the subject of concern to American businessmen, are in the short run at most a partial offset to the direct effect of higher US service exports. Thus liberalization of any existing barriers in Japan to the services of foreign financial institutions would be not only as beneficial for the efficient global allocation of economic resources, but also as popular in the United States, as liberalization of quotas in Japan on imports of beef and citrus. More precisely, such measures are popular with US bankers and farmers, respectively. Morgan Guaranty's *World Financial Markets* (June 1984, p. 11) says, "If it is true that Japan enjoys an enduring comparative advantage in manufacturing, it follows that others have a comparative advantage in the field of financial and other services." However, one point usually escapes attention: measures to increase Japanese imports of banking services are *not* in the interest of US manufacturers, such as Caterpillar Tractor, which will have to compete against even more competitively priced Japanese exports if the yen depreciates further.

As Pigott (1983, pp. 40–41) explains, the 1979–80 period of liberalization "effectively extended to foreign banks treatment equal to that of their Japanese counterparts," by giving them increased access to sources of funds, including a new market in CDs and the Bank of Japan's discount window. Indeed, foreign banks may in some respects now be treated better than Japanese banks.[54] The May Yen/Dollar Group report (p. 21) reaffirmed the commitment of both sides to the principle of national treatment, that is, equal treatment for domestic and foreign banks in Japan.

ESTABLISHMENT OF FOREIGN BRANCHES IN JAPAN

Foreign banks and other financial institutions are free to acquire subsidiaries in Japan. There are currently about 30 US banks operating there.[55] However,

---

54. Hamada (1984, p. 10) says "At least formally, foreign bankers are now given almost equal or even preferential treatment in its operations compared with Japanese bankers." American banks have mixed feelings about joining the banking fraternity in Japan because membership has in the past carried the obligation to accept an allocated share of government bonds at below-market interest rates.

55. *American Banker*, 12 June 1984. According to Sakakibara and Kondoh (1984, p. 51), there are 210 branches and representative offices of foreign banks in Japan (as of September 1983) and 84 of foreign securities companies (as of the end of 1982).

the US side in the negotiations registered complaints regarding the difficulty of the application process for foreign securities firms. During the period October 1983 to February 1984, Goldman Sachs, Citicorp, and Security Pacific each acquired branches in Japan.

LIMITS ON SWAP LOANS

One form of control maintained by the Ministry of Finance up to 1983 was a limit on the amount of foreign currency that each foreign and Japanese bank could convert into yen for the purpose of lending in Japan. Murchison and Solomon (pp. 63–64, 109) urge that all such restrictions, known as swap limits, be removed.

The 1983 GAO study (p. 48) finds that the swap limits were "not a factor during the period we reviewed, since the banks were not fully using their allotted quotas." Nevertheless, the limits may have had some effect because banks seek to hold a margin of reserves. In any case, the Ministry of Finance in December raised the limits on foreign banks. Subsequently, in the Yen/Dollar Working Group (p. 17), the ministry agreed to remove all swap limits for both Japanese and foreign banks, effective June 1, 1984.

MANAGEMENT OF TRUST FUNDS

A more substantive issue is the entry of foreign banks into the business of managing trust and pension funds in Japan. This business is expected to become increasingly important as the population ages. So far, it has been the exclusive province of Japanese trust banks and life insurance companies.

In May the Yen/Dollar Working Group (p. 22) agreed on a "new policy to license qualified foreign banks to participate in the same range of trust banking activities. . . ." A concrete scheme is to be announced and to take effect by 1985. This would place foreign banks in a better position than that class of Japanese banks currently excluded. At least four US banks announced plans to form joint ventures with a corresponding Japanese securities company to enter the trust business, but Ministry of Finance approval was denied in May.[56] Only joint ventures with Japanese trust banks are permitted (in

---

56. *Yomiuri*, 9 May 1984.

addition to ventures by foreign banks alone, which are less likely to be attempted, Freeman, p. A6).

DEALING IN JAPANESE GOVERNMENT BONDS

Several US banks and several foreign securities companies were granted membership in the underwriting syndicate that sells newly issued government bonds, effective April 1, 1984, with as many more on the way. Membership requires monthly purchases of new government issues, traditionally at below-market rates, but also allows resale of the bonds after a 100-day holding period (Freeman, p. A8). Apparently, the Ministry of Finance is in the process of allowing the banks to trade *outstanding* government bonds as well (Sakakibara and Kondoh, p. 16, n. 5).

MEMBERSHIP IN THE TOKYO STOCK EXCHANGE

Americans have complained that the ownership of seats on the stock exchange is limited to Japanese. In the Yen/Dollar Working Group (p. 21), the Ministry of Finance replied that there are no rules against foreign membership (such rules having been dropped since the time that Secretary Regan was chairman at Merrill-Lynch), that the Tokyo Stock Exchange is an autonomous institution and that, although no seats have been offered for sale recently, the government cannot force the exchange to provide seats. However, the Japanese did agree that non-Japanese membership is desirable, and requested the exchange to study ways to make a seat available. It is understood that the study began in July.

6   Liberalization of Domestic Capital Markets

Of the four categories of measures, domestic liberalization might be considered the most likely to have a significant upward effect on the yen, and to have beneficial implications for the efficient and equitable working of the Japanese economy.[57] But domestic liberalization is already taking place at a deliberate pace and is the category of policy measures least susceptible to being speeded up in response to US pressure.

In the past, virtually all interest rates in Japan were fixed administratively, in effect by the government. As in most countries, the higher rate of inflation in the 1970s, consisting primarily of the 1973–74 oil shock episode in the case of Japan, implied low or negative real interest rates. In the United States, the resulting disintermediation forced increasing flexibility of interest rates, as represented for example by the growth of money market funds and NOW accounts, the payment of competitive interest rates on US savings bonds, the phasing out of Regulation Q, and the spread of adjustable rate mortgages. In Japan a similar process is taking place, but with quite a lag.

In the late 1970s interest rates were significantly deregulated in short-term money markets. While participation in the call market (one- to seven-day funds, as in the US federal funds markets) and bill market is limited to banks,[58] other institutions can participate in the CD and gensaki markets.

However, longer term securities markets are not well-developed and are largely dominated by government financing.[59] Liberalization in the primary market for government securities is in its early stages. Deregulation of interest rates paid to depositors and other individual investors has hardly begun. Freeman (p. 9) concludes:

While the freeing of interest rates in money markets and the development of an active secondary market in government bonds represent a significant movement toward full liberalization of domestic markets, it is still the case that the vast majority of deposit and lending rates in Japan are not determined by market forces with full flexibility.

---

57. This, for example, is the view of *The Economist*. Saxonhouse (1983b, p. 293) argues, "the lack of full liberalization at home . . . ." defined as the creation of financial instruments, available domestically and internationally, at market-determined prices, "works to depress the value of the yen."

58. Sakakibara and Kondoh (1984, pp. vi, xiii, 4–6, 25) note that the call and bill discount "markets" in fact consist of a cartel of six money dealers, and challenge statements made by the Bank of Japan in the Yen/Dollar Working Group that it does not exercise close guidance.

59. Freeman (1984, p. A4); Eken (forthcoming, p. 10); Sakakibara and Kondoh (1984, pp. x, 13).

Measures to Liberalize Domestic Markets

To the extent that government regulation has kept interest rates in Japan lower than they would otherwise be, it has encouraged net capital outflow and weakened the yen. Murchison and Solomon (pp. 107–9) urge a whole range of measures to free up interest rates and otherwise liberalize Japanese domestic capital markets. Some, like the possible establishment of a banker's acceptance market, have already been discussed; but three areas remain.

BANK CERTIFICATES OF DEPOSIT

Negotiable CDs were originally introduced in 1979 in response to pressure partly from Japanese banks, partly from abroad. Murchison and Solomon (p. 109) propose that the denomination be decreased, to make them more accessible to small investors, and that ceilings on how much each bank could issue be eliminated. The November Regan-Takeshita announcement incorporated steps in both directions. Effective January 1, 1984, the Ministry of Finance lowered the minimum denomination of CDs from ¥500 million to ¥300 million. Effective the second quarter, it began enlarging the ceilings, previously at 75 percent of net worth for domestic banks, eventually to reach 100 percent. Similar ceiling enlargements were enacted for foreign banks (Pigott, p. 33; GAO, pp. 24–25).

Those changes were not enough to make the CD market relevant for small savers or enough to elicit at first a noticeable increase in CD activity.[60] In the Yen/Dollar report (p. 14), the Ministry of Finance agreed to seek to lower the minimum denomination further to ¥100 million over the subsequent year, to enlarge further the bank ceilings, and also to relax restrictions on banks' large-denomination deposit instruments.

GOVERNMENT SECURITIES

The Japanese government first began to run large budget deficits in the mid-1970s, in part to absorb the emerging excess of saving over investment.[61]

---

60. The points are made by Hamada (1984, p. 13) and *Euromoney* (1984), respectively.
61. GAO (1984, p. 51); Freeman (1984, p. 5); Pigott (1983, p. 29); Eken (forthcoming, p. 4); *World Financial Markets* (June 1984), p. 4; Suzuki (1984, p. 3); Yoshitomi (1984a, p. 18; 1984b, pp. 9–10); Sakakibara and Kondoh (1984, pp. xviii, 1).

Banks became unenthusiastic about their obligation to buy government bonds that occupied an increasingly large share of bank portfolios, from 2.2 percent of total assets at the end of 1975 to 7.8 percent at the end of 1978.[62] In April 1981, sometime after a secondary market began to develop, the minimum period for which banks were required to hold government bonds before reselling them on the secondary market was reduced. But the losses incurred by the banks, forced to buy the bonds at below-market rates, became that much more obvious. As a result, the system came under increasing strain. Members of the syndicate on occasion refused to buy the bonds (GAO, p. 53).

In 1979 the government began to raise the interest rate at which the banks were asked to buy the issues. Since late 1982 the interest rate at issue has been adjusted frequently in response to changes in market interest rates.[63] In October 1983 banks were allowed to sell medium-term government bonds over the counter.[64] The Yen/Dollar report (p. 15) noted that, as of June 1, 1984, qualified Japanese banks can buy and sell government securities in the secondary market, and anticipated that non-Japanese banks would soon be allowed to do the same.

There has been no traditional market in short-term government securities analogous to the US Treasury bill market. Almost all have been sold to the Bank of Japan, as "cash-management notes." In recent years the Bank of Japan has undertaken some sales of short-term government securities. But the market is still very limited.[65] Expansion of the Treasury bill market is another Murchison-Solomon (p. 109) proposal. It has been pointed out that the large number of 10-year government bonds issued beginning around 1975 have increasingly short terms left to maturity, so that their secondary market is a de facto short-term market.[66] With the release of the Yen/Dollar report, the US Treasury registered failure at persuading the Japanese side to change its system of cash-management notes.[67] But the Ministry of Finance is studying the subject of a market in short-term government debt.[68]

---

62. OECD *Economic Survey* (July 1984), p. 47.

63. *Ibid.*, p. 47.

64. *Ibid.*, p. 80; Suzuki (1984, p. 10).

65. Sakakibara and Kondoh (1984, p. ii) point out that the Bank of Japan does not conduct open market sales, but rather sells the short-term government securities to a cartel of six dealers.

66. GAO (1984, p. 53); Yen/Dollar Working Group (1984, p. 15); OECD (1984, p. 49); Yoshitomi (1984a, p. 20); Sakakibara and Kondoh (1984, pp. ii, xiv).

67. Yen/Dollar Working Group (1984, p. 15); Rowen (1984, p. A1).

68. Freeman (1984, p. A9); Yen/Dollar Working Group (1984, p. 15); Sakakibara and Kondoh (1984, pp. xiv, 28).

HOUSEHOLDS' DEPOSITS

Less liberalization in assets available to small investors has taken place than in any other area. Most interest rates paid on bank deposits and in the large Postal Savings System are still fixed at low levels. This arrangement impairs both efficiency, with respect to the Japanese economy, and equity, with respect to the wealth of the investor, much as Regulation Q did in the United States until recently.

Since the 1970s, automated teller machines and similar arrangements have allowed Japanese residents to economize on currency holdings. An analogue to NOW or sweep accounts in the United States has also developed: sogokoza, which allow investment accounts to perform transaction functions by serving as collateral for automatically granted overdrafts of demand deposit accounts (Suzuki, p. 13). Recently, joint ventures between a credit association and a securities fund have been formed for similar purposes. Other arrangements are also in the works.[69]

The Order of Liberalization

The US campaign has undoubtedly speeded up the process of domestic financial market liberalization in Japan to a certain degree. The vision of "step-by-step" liberalization has given way to the metaphor of "advancing by long strides."[70] But Japan has made clear that it wants to proceed at its own deliberate pace and not to be pushed into "running" by the United States.

How does the desirable speed of domestic liberalization compare with the desirable speed of international liberalization? There exists a substantial body of theoretical literature, inspired by the Southern Cone countries of Latin America (Argentina, Chile, and Uruguay), on the subject of the optimal order of liberalization. The consensus in this literature is that domestic capital markets should be liberalized *before* international capital markets, so that capital flows with the rest of the world do not respond to rates of return that are incorrect signals for the best long-run allocation of capital.[71] In Latin

---

69. Freeman (1984, pp. A7–A8) refers to money market certificates.

70. Interview with Oba, *Look Japan*, 10 July 1984.

71. See Edwards (1983) and the other references cited there. McKinnon (1983a, p. 369; 1983b) is one who believes that domestic interest rates should be allowed to rise before capital controls are removed.

America in the late 1970s, the problem was capital inflow in response to interest rates above the US level. In Japan in the 1980s, the context is quite different; the problem is capital outflow in response to interest rates below the US level. But, if decreasing the yen/dollar exchange rate is the goal, the lesson is the same. Liberalization of international flows before domestic deregulation will clearly operate in the opposite direction from that desired.

The Bank of Japan has stated the position that the liberalization of domestic financial markets should come first.[72] A possible response is that the Japanese position is a delaying tactic. Some observers are advocating international liberalization, particularly in the Euro-yen market, precisely because it will force more rapid liberalization of interest rates within Japan as Japanese borrowers are forced to compete on world capital markets (Hamada, p. 13). The outcome of the sequence question seems to be that international liberalization is proceeding somewhat in advance of domestic liberalization.[73]

It also seems that within the range of measures promoting domestic liberalization, interest rates paid to financial intermediaries (whether by the government, private business, or other financial intermediaries) are being raised faster than interest rates paid by financial intermediaries to individual savers.[74] This has been the pattern in many other countries as well. With respect to capital outflow from Japan and the effect on the exchange rate, one could argue that if an investor is too small to buy a CD, then he or she is too small to buy foreign securities, no matter how much the government liberalizes. The implication would be that there is no need to pay competitive rates on households' deposits. But once one recognizes that the cost of capital faced by Japanese businesses and the government is being raised to world levels, it is especially hard to argue that financial intermediaries should be allowed to pay lower interest rates so that they can be subsidized by small

---

72. *Look Japan*, 10 July 1984, p. 8.

73. Deputy Finance Minister Oba is cited as saying that liberalization will proceed more slowly in domestic capital markets than internationally; for example, *New York Times*, 30 May. This characterization is expressed also in *Look Japan*, 10 July 1984, p. 8, and by Freeman (1984, p. 9), who suggests that Japanese authorities may be using international liberalization as a "testing area for possible reforms."

74. On the other hand, *World Financial Markets* (June 1984), p. 6: "It has been commonly assumed that decontrol of large deposits, those most vulnerable to competition from rival instruments, would precede the freeing of small deposits. However this may not be so, given the tangle of political and bureaucratic vested interests. . . ."

savers. As Hamada (p. 18) puts it, "Deregulation should come not for the sake of the yen or American deficits, but for the sake of its benefit to the Japanese economy, and particularly to Japanese consumers."

7   Public Reaction to the Liberalization of October 1983–May 1984

Reactions in the Media

While the Yen/Dollar negotiations were underway, journalistic coverage in the United States was for the most part limited to the straightforward reporting of Treasury officials' public statements. But when the agreement was completed and the report released on May 29, most observers whose opinion was sought out took the line that the measures were unlikely to have a large effect on the yen/dollar rate.

Such observers fell into several categories. First were those who repeated earlier claims that the Japanese promises were not meaningful, and would not result in significant changes in the structure of capital markets. A column by Lester Thurow under the headline "Yanks Hoodwinked Again" represents an extreme example:

The Reagan Administration spent almost four years yelling during negotiations but, at the end, got a minuscule change in the Japanese financial system . . . [T]he negotiated changes are so modest and so spread out over three years that it is clear they will do little to raise the value of the yen. Once again Americans have been out-negotiated by the Japanese.[75]

---

75. *Boston Globe*, 5 June 1984, p. 28. Similar reactions appear in a *Business Week* editorial 11 June, "The Yen and Yang of the Yen Accord"; an *Economist* 2 June editorial "Yen for Reform," p. 16; *USA Today*, 30 May, "Yen's Value May Dip Early"; and *Financial Times*, 30 May, "Japan, US Agree on Yen Package."

Similarly, *World Financial Markets* (June 1984, p. 9) commented: "the contrast between vigorous outflows and sluggish inflows gives some credence to foreign suspicions that Japan has managed its external liberalization in a way that depresses the yen's exchange value and thereby maintains unfair competitive advantage for Japanese business." But capital flows cannot be taken ex post as evidence on whether liberalization discriminates against outflow. We saw in section 3 that in the aftermath of the 1979–80 liberalization, capital began to flow out of Japan on balance, even though controls on *inflow* had been liberalized the most. If net capital outflow is taken as evidence that Japanese policy is responsible, then by analogy, from the fact that the United States imports large amounts of textiles, it could be inferred that US policy subsidizes textile imports. Or from the fact that Japan is America's largest customer of agricultural products it could be inferred that Japanese policy subsidizes agricultural imports. In both cases, market factors are a more obvious cause: higher interest rates in the United States than in Japan, in the case of capital flows; comparative advantage, in the case of trade flows. Sometimes government intervention determines economic outcomes, but often it is at most a partially mitigating factor in opposition to more powerful market forces. The recent period of capital outflows from Japan and inflows to the United States is such a case.

The second major category of reactions, in the author's view correct in their evaluation, came from those who agreed that major changes would occur in the structure of Japanese capital markets but who judged that they would have no large effect on the exchange rate, except perhaps in the long run or in the wrong direction.[76] The clearest and strongest statements to appear were made by C. Fred Bergsten (1984, p. 4), who testified, "the recently announced US-Japan 'yen agreement' will make the problem worse, at least in the short run, by encouraging more capital outflow from Japan."

Occasionally a third argument is given to explain why, even if major changes are implemented quickly, and even if they raise the value of the yen

---

76. *Washington Post*, 23 May 1984, "The Yen to Travel"; *Wall Street Journal*, 29 May, "US Japan Pact Won't Spur Fast Rise in Yen"; *Boston Globe*, 31 May, "Cracking the Yen Cocoon"; 5 July, "Impact of Yen Accord Disappointing Thus Far." A June 11 *Business Week* story "The Yen May Turn Out to be a Paper Tiger," p. 42, had a different thrust from the editorial in the same issue; it reported some US officials as believing that the agreement will bring as much as a 10 percent to 15 percent appreciation in the yen, but reported the consensus elsewhere to be, if anything, an opposite effect.

quickly, there may be no quick improvement in the US trade balance with Japan. The argument is that after a dollar depreciation it takes one year or so before the reactions in import and export demand are great enough that the sum of their elasticities exceeds one, and so outweigh the negative valuation effect from higher import prices; this implies that the effect on the trade balance in the first year is not positive. The problem with this argument lies precisely in the fact, discussed in section 4, that not only 97 percent of Japanese imports but also 60 percent of exports are invoiced in foreign currency rather than yen. For those categories of goods invoiced only in dollars, trade elasticities need only be greater than zero for a positive effect on the bilateral US-Japan monthly trade balance, even in the short run.[77]

Treasury officials, while describing the Yen/Dollar Working Group report as a "historic agreement," agreed that the yen would not necessarily appreciate in the short run. But, they maintained, as the demand for yen increases over time in response to the internationalization measures, there will be a significant long-run upward effect on the value of the yen. Exchange rates are determined by many unpredictable factors. It may be that no one will ever be able to tell whether the value of the yen is higher on account of the 1984 liberalization than it would otherwise have been. But we now turn to an attempt to measure the effect statistically.

Reactions in the Market

If economic wisdom ultimately resides in the private marketplace, and not in the government, then it is logical to look to the foreign exchange markets for a possible judgment on the campaign for yen/dollar liberalization. By October 1984, the yen had depreciated 6 percent against the dollar, relative to its level before the first set of liberalization steps was announced one year earlier (¥231.75/$1 at 2 P.M. EST October 20, 1983, which in Tokyo was early on the day that the Fiscal Year 1984 omnibus bill was revealed). Of course many other factors moved the yen/dollar rate during that period. For

---

77. The J-curve argument is attributed to American officials (as an admission) in *Newsweek*, 11 June 1984 "Muscling the Yen to the Mat," and in *Washington Post*, 30 May, p. A20, "US, Japan Set Major Yen Accord." Also the *Journal of Commerce*, 24 July, "Japanese Port Traffic Lags Growth in Trade," pp. A1, A12, states that a depreciation of the yen improves Japanese competitiveness *specifically because* most of Japan's trade is conducted in dollar terms!

example, the US-Japan nominal interest differential rose another point or so, and the real interest differential probably rose similarly. But if we look at the market reaction just on the day when the Working Group's report was released (May 29, 1984), and on each of the days over the preceding seven months when news about the yen/dollar campaign occurred, we can hope to isolate the effect of the news on the exchange rate.[78]

This still leaves the problem that the hypothesis claimed by Treasury is not that the liberalization measures will raise demand for yen in the short run, but only that they will do so in the long run. A first step toward getting around this problem is to realize that we can look at the reaction in the forward exchange rate. The theory of efficient markets tells us that the forward exchange rate should correctly reflect all publicly available information that is relevant to the expected value of the future spot exchange rate.[79] The forward rate data used are the longest maturity available: one year.

Table 7 presents the results for the reaction of the spot rate in percentages (logarithmic). The first five rows show the reactions to the five most important developments between October 1983 and June 1984: respectively, the release in Tokyo of the omnibus bill, the Regan-Takeshita announcement in Tokyo, the beginning of 1984 when some of the measures took effect, the beginning of the second quarter when many of the other measures took effect, and the release of the Yen/Dollar report in Washington. The reactions are evenly split between positive and negative. It is not terribly surprising that there is no large or systematic effect: each of these five events was known ahead of time, and had presumably already been discounted by the market.

---

78. Empirical studies on the effect of "news" are common in the exchange rate literature. Two examples are Jacob Frenkel (1981) and Engel and Frankel (1984).

79. The forward rate need not equal the expected future spot rate if there are significant barriers to capital movement, i.e., markets are not efficient or there is a non-zero risk premium. Even if the first condition were believed to apply to the Tokyo forward exchange market, it does not apply to New York, from where our data are taken. The empirical evidence on the existence of a risk premium has not yet reached a consensus. (See Frankel [1982b] for references.) But there is a consensus that the risk premium is in any case probably small, and there is no obvious reason to think it would react systematically to news on the yen/dollar liberalization. Ito (1984) statistically does not reject the joint hypothesis of market efficiency and a zero risk premium for the yen/dollar exchange rate, using data on three-month interest rates both in Japan and offshore.

TABLE 7 **Reaction of spot dollar/yen rate to news**
(as logarithmic percentage of level)

News	One-day change			Two-day change			Sample size
1. Oct. 21, 1983	+.09			−.37			1
2. Nov. 10, 1983	+.38			−.00			1
3. Jan. 1, 1984	+.02			−.91			1
4. Apr. 1, 1984	−.20			−.16			1
5. May 29, 1984	−.09			+.19			1
	Mean	*Variance*[a]	*t-ratio*	*Mean*	*Variance*[a]	*t-ratio*	
6. US	+.22	3.4	+1.188	+.12	4.2	+0.565	14
7. JNEWS	+.072	1.9	+0.522	+.25	5.7	+1.045	18
8. JEVENT	+.029	0.37	+0.484	+.059	0.42	+0.908	39
9. JDOMESTIC	+.19	5.4	+0.823	+.589	13.0	+1.580	11
10. NEGATIVE	+.014	1.4	+0.119	+.86	4.4	+0.412	5
OVERALL (1–9)	+.10	0.40	+1.625	+.100	0.75	+1.155	64

Note: A given day is counted only once in each category, which is why the overall sample size is less than the sum of the sizes of subsamples 1–8.
Source: Data Resources, Inc.
a. Variance of the change *times* 10 to the 10th.

The next five rows show the reactions to categories of lesser developments. The first category ("US") is news released in the United States either as a US government announcement, American newspaper reporting of a specific event, or a general news story on the yen/dollar campaign in a major American periodical. The second category ("JNEWS") is Japanese newspaper reporting of specific events regarding the liberalization. The third category ("JEVENT") is actual events in Japan themselves regarding the liberalization: either Japanese government announcements, the taking effect of minor previously announced measures, or other actions. The fourth category ("JDOMESTIC," overlapping with the second and third) is all news or government announcements in Japan that relate specifically to the liberalization of *domestic* financial markets. In section 6 such measures were argued to have the best chance of affecting the exchange rate in the desired direction. The fifth category ("NEGATIVE") is those developments that appeared to indicate low-points in relations between the two sides in the negotiations; under the Treasury hypothesis, the yen might be expected to weaken on such days.[80]

First, we look at the one-day change (from mid-day New York time, which is early the next day Tokyo time, to the same time one working day later). The effects are positive, indicating an appreciation of the yen, but none is statistically significant at the 95 percent level, as indicated by the t-ratio. Then we look at the two-day change, because in some cases it may take an extra day before events are publicly known. It shows results similar to the one-day change. In both cases the reaction to news regarding domestic liberalization is stronger than to the other categories, as hypothesized, but is still not statistically greater than zero. Our best chance for significant results is to add together all 64 observations (excluding only those relating to news considered negative to the campaign). Although this does raise the magnitude of the t-statistic, the effect is still not statistically significant. But if the effect is in fact there, the total impact of the campaign on the exchange rate is an estimated 6.6 percent ($= .10 \times 64$).

Table 8 presents the results of the reactions of the forward rate to the same sets of events. They are more favorable to the Treasury hypothesis than the results for the spot rate. None of the categories shows a statistically significant effect, but when all observations are added together, the one-day change is significant at the 95 percent confidence level. The total effect of the campaign from October 1983 to June 1984 is estimated at 8.2 percent ($= .13 \times 64$). This is quite a bit larger than expected. Evidently the market believed the statements of Treasury officials, which in US newspapers up until May 1984

---

80. The five categories of observation dates are as follows. Obviously these lists cannot claim to be an utterly exhaustive compilation of all relevant events and news stories. In the tables, one-day and two-day changes refer to business days; where more than one event date falls on the same weekend, the number of dates listed here will exceed the sample size given in the tables.

US: 12/29/83, 1/26/84, 3/5, 3/30, 4/2, 4/13, 4/17, 4/22, 5/20, 5/21, 5/23, 5/24, 6/1, 6/4, 6/5, 6/11.

JNEWS: 10/27/83, 2/28/84, 3/3, 3/7, 3/27, 3/28, 3/30, 3/31, 4/6, 4/10, 4/15, 4/20, 4/21, 4/28, 4/29, 5/2, 5/3, 5/13, 5/25, 5/30.

JEVENT: 10/13/83, 10/25, 11/1, 11/14, 11/15, 11/16, 11/24, 11/30, 12/15, 12/21, 12/22, 12/23, 1/27/84, 1/31, 2/10, 2/21, 2/27, 2/28, 3/19, 3/22, 3/27, 3/28, 3/29, 3/30, 4/6, 4/9, 4/10, 4/17, 4/18, 4/19, 4/28, 5/1, 5/10, 5/11, 5/12, 5/15, 5/18, 5/25, 5/29, 6/1.

JDOMESTIC: 11/30/83, 12/21, 12/22, 12/23, 3/3/84, 3/28, 4/6, 4/9, 4/10, 4/28, 4/29.

NEGATIVE: 2/23/84, 2/24, 2/25, 3/9, 3/24, 4/18.

TABLE 8   **Reaction of one-year forward dollar/yen rate to news**
(as logarithmic percentage of level)

News	One-day change			Two-day change			Sample size
1. Oct. 21, 1983	+.09			−.32			1
2. Nov. 10, 1983	+.41			−.091			1
3. Jan. 1, 1984	+.09			−.87			1
4. Apr. 1, 1984	−.26			−.11			1
5. May 29, 1984	−.17			+.24			1
	Mean	Variance[a]	t-ratio	Mean	Variance[a]	t-ratio	
6. US	+.21	3.7	+1.102	+.13	4.2	+0.613	14
7. JNEWS	+.11	1.8	+0.807	+.31	5.7	+1.318	18
8. JEVENT	+.062	0.33	+1.089	+.094	0.42	+1.447	39
9. JDOMESTIC	+.19	5.0	+0.829	+.60	13.0	+1.648	11
10. NEGATIVE	+.031	1.1	+0.292	+.12	3.7	+0.624	5
OVERALL (1–9)	+.13	0.40	+2.064	+.14	0.75	+1.619	64

Note: A given day is counted only once in each category, which is why the overall sample size is less than the sum of the sizes of subsamples 1–8.
Source: Data Resources, Inc.
a. Variance of the change *times* 10 to the 10th.

constituted the dominant source of information, that the measures would be likely to appreciate the yen.

It can be argued that our estimates of the effect on the spot and one-year forward rates are upper bounds on the true long-run effect. Imagine constructing surrogate long-term forward rates by using data on long-term interest rates and using the covered interest-parity relationship, which tells us that the forward rate *is equal* to the spot rate *plus* the interest rate differential. If one admits that an immediate effect of the liberalization is to allow more capital to flow out of Japan in response to the higher long-run interest rate available in New York, then one must admit that the US-Japan long-term interest differential will, if anything, immediately fall. In any case, reducing the US-Japan interest differential is certainly an objective of those measures dealing with liberalization of Japan's domestic financial markets. But then the increase in the spot or one-year forward dollar/yen rate will, if anything, *overstate* the rise in the long-term forward rate. In other words our results will be biased in favor of the Treasury hypothesis. (However, if one believes that the interest differential widened, then our results will be biased against the Treasury hypothesis.)

8 The Current Account and Saving in Japan, Again

We found in section 2 that the trade-weighted value of the yen has not declined relative to its average over the period since 1973. Such calculations presume that the "correct" equilibrium value of the exchange rate manifests itself in long-run averages. Some Americans claim that the yen has *always* been "undervalued." Such statements essentially amount to the proposition that Japan has a current account surplus that is persistently too high, whatever the exchange rate. Some American businessmen probably feel that any value of the dollar/yen rate is too low if their companies have trouble competing with Japanese exporters.

Having examined the effects on the exchange rate, it is worthwhile going beyond them to look at effects on the current account, which is after all the ultimate object of concern. For example, we noted in section 5 that measures pertaining to the promotion of American financial services in Japan would have a positive effect on the US current account, even if a further effect is to depreciate the yen.

As noted in section 2, Japan ran a current account surplus equal to 1.8 percent of GNP in 1983, and the OECD forecasts that in 1984 it will be 2.4 percent of GNP. While industrial countries are on average expected to run current account surpluses, the recent Japanese numbers are high. The United States ran a current account deficit equal to 1.2 percent of GNP in 1983 and is expected to register a deficit of about 3.0 percent in 1984. Of course, the strong dollar has a lot to do with the US deficits; from 1971 to 1981, when the dollar was much weaker, the United States was on average in balance. But even the European Community's surplus was only 0.1 percent of GNP in 1983, and is forecast to be only 0.2 percent in 1984.[81] Why is the recent Japanese current account surplus so much bigger?

It is useful to think of the balance of payments in terms of saving and investment. By identity, a country's current account surplus *is equal* to its total national saving, public and private, *minus* its investment. In 1982, gross national saving in Japan was 30.8 percent of GDP, while in the United States it was only 15.9 percent of GNP. Investment was also higher in Japan, but not by quite as much.[82] For each country the discrepancy is the current account: the surplus for Japan and the deficit for the United States. One way to think of it is that in autarky (i.e., in the hypothetical absence of international transactions) Japan's excess of saving would cause its real interest rate to be relatively low, and the United States' deficiency of saving would cause its real interest rate to be relatively high. It follows that when the countries are able to trade goods and capital with each other, the market equilibrium is a net capital flow from Japan to the United States.[83]

While the high personal saving rate in Japan is attributed largely to cultural factors, government policy works in a number of ways to increase national saving relative to policy in the United States. The tax code exempts interest

81. Figures are from the OECD *Economic Outlook* (July 1984), pp. 35, 132, except for the 1984 US deficit, which is the author's estimate.
82. Gross fixed capital formation in 1982 was 29.9 percent of GDP in Japan and 16.6 in the United States (OECD, 1984, pp. 154–55). In the fourth quarter of 1982, at the trough of the recession, US national saving net of depreciation (as measured by the Council of Economic Advisers) was actually a negative number. (In other words, the capital stock would have been shrinking had it not been for a capital inflow from abroad.) Since then, national saving has increased rapidly. But as of mid-1984, it was still lower as a percentage of GNP than it was in the 1950s, 1960s, or 1970s, and is increasing less rapidly than national investment, i.e., the current account deficit is widening. While Japan is a net creditor vis-à-vis the rest of the world, the United States will become a net debtor in early 1985.
83. The characterization of Japan as a country where high national saving keeps real interest rates low has been more than hypothetical for most of the postwar period. However, as pointed out in footnote 14, Japanese real interest rates in recent years have by many measures been the second highest among major industrial countries, after the United States. One explanation is the recent tendency, discussed in section 2, for the Japanese monetary authorities to keep interest rates higher than they would otherwise be, in order to keep the yen from depreciating. Another factor may be that Europe in the aggregate has, like Japan, been reducing its structural budget deficit; Germany and the United Kingdom had actually attained structural budget surpluses by 1983. Only the United States has moved sharply in the opposite direction. The statistics are in Muller and Price (1984).

income from the first 3 million yen of savings deposits in a bank account or Postal Savings Account (the "maruyu" system). The social security system up until now has taken in more than it has paid out. The availability of mortgages and other consumer credit is limited; in 1982 outstanding consumer credit was only about 1 percent of private consumption, compared with almost 8 percent in the United States.[84] These incentives to save have no doubt contributed to Japan's ability to maintain relatively low real interest rates in the past and to its current account surplus. But such policies, by the professed standards of the US administration and many others, are considered worthy of praise, not blame. As *World Financial Markets* (p. 11) puts it:

Japan's partners—especially the United States and the EC—should recognize that their trade differences with Japan, while sometimes stemming from unequal competitive conditions, more often reflect their own deficient savings and laggardly restructuring by their own industries. Often, their savings are hampered by lax budget policies and fiscal disincentives. By contrast, Japan has consistently encouraged high personal savings through tax and institutional incentives.

What effect will the 1984 liberalization of Japanese capital markets have on saving and investment in Japan? The clearest effect will be increased efficiency in the allocation of saving among its possible uses. But for the determination of the current account, it is the overall *levels* of saving and investment that matter. On this it is more difficult to say. Few of the measures taken directly concern incentives to save and invest in Japan.

Some observers might argue that firms will have to adjust to a higher cost of capital—the world real interest rate—than they are accustomed to. This would tend to reduce their level of investment and thus, all else remaining the same, *increase* the Japanese current account surplus, whatever happens to the exchange rate. However, most such adjustment had in any case already taken place by 1983.

It is more certain that, as domestic liberalization proceeds in Japan, the interest rate received by households on their deposits will rise, toward the market-clearing levels that banks and other large investors have already won for themselves. Saving more is one possible response by households to the enhanced rate of return. This effect, again, would work to increase the

---

84. Hama (1983, p. 24); Fukao (1984, pp. 16–17); *World Financial Markets* (June 1984), pp. 2, 5, and Solomon (1983, pp. 92, 96–97). The consumer credit statistics are from OECD *Economic Survey of Japan* (July 1984), p. 53.

Japanese current account surplus (Yoshitomi 1984, p. 97). However, the implication of increased saving rates need not follow from the higher rate of return. According to economic theory, the effect depends on opposing substitution and income effects. On the one hand, households will want to substitute future consumption for current consumption when the reward for doing so is greater, which will tend to raise saving today. On the other hand, with the increased rate of return, they now do not have to save as much today to attain a given level of consumption tomorrow.

The empirical evidence on the responsiveness of saving to the rate of return is at best mixed, even for the United States. In the case of Japan, it has been argued that the supply of saving is especially steep and may even be backward-bending, on the grounds that Japanese households are target-savers: the paramount concern is attaining a given-sized nest egg to buy housing, so that an increase in the rate of return, which makes this easier, allows the household to save less and consume more today.[85] On balance, the net effect of the liberalization package on Japan's saving-investment gap, and thus on its current account surplus, seems more likely to be upward rather than downward. But like the net effect on the exchange rate, it seems likely in any case to be small.

Only a fiscal expansion on the part of the Japanese government can rapidly reduce national saving and the current account surplus. One likely channel through which this result might come about would be an increase in the real interest rate in Japan, a reduction of capital outflow and, as consequences, the sought-after stronger yen and reduced Japanese trade surplus. The current US administration is not inclined to urge this course on Japan. Under Secretary Sprinkel has testified:

We should not press Japan to reorient its fiscal and monetary policy toward relaxing efforts to control budget deficits and raising Japanese interest rates. The Japanese authorities want to cut fiscal deficits and the growth in government expenditures. These are the same fiscal objectives this Administration is pursuing. I would not accept contrary advice for the United States.[86]

It is a short step to the conclusion that the key to solving the problem of the low dollar/yen exchange rate and consequent trade imbalance is for the United States to act firmly to reduce its own federal budget deficit. Such action

---

85. The target-savers argument is made by Saxonhouse (1982, 1983a) and Sato (1982).
86. Congressional testimony, 30 November 1982, quoted by Hama (1983, p. 48).

would help bring down US real interest rates and reduce the net flow of capital from Japan to the United States, even while each country benefits from increasing gross flows of capital and goods in both directions across the Pacific.

9   Conclusions

In conclusion, we summarize nine points made in this paper.

- The yen is not especially undervalued. Only the European currencies have depreciated sharply since 1980. It is more accurate to describe the dollar as overvalued than the yen as undervalued.

- To the extent that Japanese capital controls were retained after 1980, they were more a force in restraint of capital outflow, and therefore in restraint of depreciation of the yen, than the reverse.

- The campaign the US Treasury launched in October 1983 had attained its immediate purpose by May 1984: adoption by the Japanese government of a variety of liberalization measures, which fall into four categories.

- However, the ultimate purpose was supposed to be an appreciation of the yen, and this outcome is much more in question. In particular, measures in the first category, further liberalization of international capital flows, are more likely to lead to weakening of the yen than strengthening it.

- If internationalization of the yen means an increase in worldwide demand for the yen, then it will push up the value of the yen. It is not clear whether the policy measures in this second category can succeed in accelerating the process.

- Measures in the third category, treatment of foreign financial institutions in Japan, can be thought of as promoting imports of financial services. As such, they tend to reduce the current account imbalance as desired, but also to depreciate the yen.

- Measures in the fourth category, liberalization of domestic capital markets, work in the direction of strengthening the yen, especially if the degree of openness (the first category) is taken as given. They also are highly desirable for the sake of efficiency and equity in the Japanese economy, as are most of the other measures.

- The net effect of the overall package on the value of the yen is completely ambiguous in direction, according to economic theory, and in any case likely to be small, according to most experts. Statistics show the effect of the 1983–84 yen/dollar campaign to have been an estimated 7 percent appreciation of the yen on the spot market, and an 8 percent appreciation on the forward market. Evidently, the markets initially took the statement of Treasury officials at face value. But by November 1984, the yen was 6 percent *weaker* against the dollar than it was before the campaign began.

- Capital is flowing out of Japan and into the United States, weakening the yen, strengthening the dollar, and creating record current account imbalances, primarily because real interest rates are higher in the United States than in Japan. This is in turn because national saving is much lower in the United States than in Japan, a divergence that the recent trends in the two countries' fiscal policies have accentuated. The yen/dollar agreement would seem to have no significant effect on the fundamental causes of the problem.

Appendices

APPENDIX A   EXCERPTS FROM HOUSE TESTIMONY, UNDER SECRETARY BERYL W. SPRINKEL

Statement of the Honorable Beryl W. Sprinkel,
Under Secretary for Monetary Affairs,
US Treasury Department,
Before the Subcommittee on Trade,
House Ways and Means Committee,

April 21, 1983

THE JAPANESE YEN EXCHANGE RATE

Mr. Chairman: I am pleased to have the opportunity to discuss again with your Subcommittee the relationship between the dollar and the Japanese yen. In my November testimony, I observed that:

> The weakening of the yen against the dollar was not unique. The dollar had appreciated against all major currencies, including the yen.

> We had found no evidence that the Japanese authorities were manipulating markets to weaken the yen. To the contrary, Japanese macroeconomic policy objectives, foreign exchange market intervention, and reluctance to lower the official discount rate all suggested that the Japanese authorities sought a stronger yen.

> Factors contributing to continued yen weakness and dollar strength included: weaker-than-expected Japanese external performance, including a decline in export volume; continued pressures in major markets for protection against Japanese exports; large capital outflows from Japan, stemming in part from recent liberalization of Japanese capital markets; continued "safe haven" demand for dollars in the face of continuing uncertainties in the international debt situation; and dramatic improvement in U.S. inflation performance. . . .

We continue to believe that differences in economic performance of the major economies are the primary factors influencing exchange rate developments; and that greater stability in exchange markets can be achieved only through greater convergence of economic policies and performance among countries. . . .

**APPENDIX B   EXCERPTS FROM MURCHISON-SOLOMON EXECUTIVE
SUMMARY, PAGES 25–27**

David C. Murchison   Ezra Solomon
Howrey and Simon   Stanford University
Washington, D.C.   Palo Alto, Ca.

*"The Misalignment of the United States Dollar and the Japanese Yen: The
Problem and Its Solution"*

Executive Summary

September 19, 1983

SUGGESTED REMEDIES

Assuming a US-Japan agreement on objectives, the following actions are available which will
lower the dollar's exchange rate, particularly against the yen, by increasing the overall
demand for yen and yen-denominated assets and reducing the overall demand for dollars and
dollar-denominated assets. President Reagan's forthcoming visit to Japan would be an ideal
time to present the following suggested list of specific measures to the Japanese Government:

1. A joint declaration by the United States and Japan that a problem exists and that the
world governments intend to work together to solve it;

2. Purchases of yen by the Federal Reserve Board in open-market transactions and in
amounts consistent with existing monetary targets. Over the past 12 months, the Federal
Reserve System, in conducting its open market operations for purposes of implementing its
chosen monetary fund targets, purchased around $15 billion of U.S. Government securities.
In the coming year, the Federal Reserve Board could allocate one-half of its desired total
purchases into yen-denominated government securities without compromising its policy goals;

3. Japanese Govenment action to convert into yen an equivalent number of dollars out of
its large holding of dollar reserves;

4. Cooperative intervention by the United States and Japan to minimize wide or precipitous
swings in exchange rates;

5. An increase in the Government of Japan's overseas borrowing with the proceeds
converted immediately into yen to assist Japan in financing its substantial budget deficits.

6. A substantial increase in the percentage of Japanese imports that are financed in yen.
Japanese importers and exporters (who jointly trade about $300 bllion a year) now denominate
a very high fraction of their invoices in U.S. dollars, thus increasing the demand for dollars.
A shift in such practices toward yen denomination will reduce world demand for dollars and
increase world demand for yen;

7. Removal of any administrative guidance restrictions which prevent full implementation of the new Japanese FOREX law;

8. Definite and specific measures by the Japanese Government to remove artificial curbs on the demand for yen, including:

  (i) removal of interest rate controls on deposits, debentures and government bonds;

  (ii) removal of constraints on short-term financial instruments such as call market, bill market, Gensaki market and certificates of deposit and expansion of the Treasury bill market;

  (iii) removal of restrictions on yen-dollar swaps;

  (iv) removal of withholding tax on non-resident interest earnings;

  (v) removal of restraints on Eurobond issues; and

  (vi) action by the Japanese Government to permit the development of an off shore banking facility.

9. The Japanese Government could take steps to increase the flow of Japanese savings into the recessed Japanese housing market;

10. Joint U.S.-Japan action to encourage other central banks which hold well over $100 billion of their reserves in dollar assets and virtually none in yen assets to buy yen and sell dollars. A $15 billion shift in the dollar-yen composition of these portfolios would increase the demand for yen and reduce the demand for dollars by $15 billion; and

11. The International Monetary Fund should review the existing misalignment of the yen and the dollar and recommend further ways to reduce the existing imbalance.

APPENDIX C   EXCERPTS FROM PRESENTATION BY
SECRETARY DONALD T. REGAN

American Center, Tokyo

Sponsored by the Keidanren

March 24, 1984

Your markets are not open to our financial institutions. Your markets are not open to the capital for the rest of the world to enjoy as is the United States market, and the message that I'm giving to your Ministry of Finance, to others, is not a new message. It's a message that

I've been delivering for three years now, and people have been saying to me: Patience, Patience. I'm about to run out of patience. I've had this now for three and a half years. How much more patience do you want? My response is: action, action, action, that's what I want now. I'm through with patience . . .

We think that the yen is probably weaker in relation to the dollar because of the fact that it's not an international currency. If there were more demand for yen, the yen would be stronger in relation to the dollar. It's not that we want to bring the dollar down or weaken the dollar. We want to bring the yen up to the dollar. We think that if there were more demand for yen that could be brought about.

Now, I just ask these gentlemen out here who import. When you import, what do you ask for in way of payment? Do you ask for yen or do you ask for dollars: Only 2 percent of Japan's imports are denominated in yen. Why? Why do you use our money? Why not your money? Why not denominate in yen? You are the second largest trading nation in the world. You should be stronger than Germany. Germans ask for D-marks, English ask for pounds, French ask for francs, yes, and the United States asks for dollars. Why does Japan ask for dollars? If you ask for yen, you would have demand for yen . . .

Now, I don't know how much you know about American advertising, but in America we have a couple of car rental companies. We have No. 1, we have No. 2, and No. 2, the Avis Company, has a slogan: "No. 2 tries harder." And we're saying if Japan is No. 2, Japan should try harder in order to become unique. The British have done it with the pound, the French have done it with the franc, the Germans have done it, the Swiss have done it. So as a result, we know the Japanese can do it if the willingness is there to do it. Sure, there is a reluctance to do it. Things are going well. Why break it up? But, on the other hand, look at it from our point of view. How can we resist the forces, the opposition party, the members of Congress, your opposite numbers who are saying: build a wall up and fence in the United States. Don't let those imports come in from other nations, whether it's the EC or Japan or where. Keep our capital at home. Don't let people borrow in our markets.

What happens, then, if we start to do that, and what I'm saying is that we have been very patient. President Reagan brought this out time and time again in meetings at Versailles at the Summit, at Williamsburg at the Summit, and then most recently again when he visited here in November. And all we keep getting is "patience, patience, you Americans are so impatient." I submit we've been very patient, extremely patient, and the time now has come, as I say, for action, action, action. . . .

References

Abegglen, James. 1983. "Is the Yen Indirectly Undervalued?" *Asian Wall Street Journal*, 4 October.

———. 1983. "Final Trade Barrier: The Price of Money." *Thinking in Writing*, II No. 30. The Boston Consulting Group, 1 March.

Atsumi, Keiko. 1984. "Vice Minister of Finance Tomomitsu Oba on Liberalization." *The Japan Economic Journal*, 3 July.

Bergsten, C. Fred. 1982. "What to Do About the US-Japan Economic Conflict." *Foreign Affairs* 60 (5): Summer, 1054–75.

———. 1984. "The United States Trade Deficit and the Dollar." Statement before the Senate Committee on Banking, Housing and Urban Affairs, Subcommittee on International Finance and Monetary Policy, Washington, 6 June.

Bergsten, C. Fred, and John Williamson. *The Multiple Reserve Currency System.* POLICY ANALYSES IN INTERNATIONAL ECONOMICS. no. 10. Washington: Institute for International Economics, forthcoming 1985.

Caterpillar Tractor Co. 1983. "Yen/Dollar Imbalance," March.

Council of Economic Advisers. 1983. *Economic Report of the President, 1983*, chap. 3. Washington, February.

———. 1984. *Economic Report of the President, 1984*, chap. 2. Washington, February.

Danker, Deborah. 1983. "Foreign Exchange Intervention, Japanese Money Markets and the Value of the Yen: A Portfolio Balance Analysis." Ph.D. diss., Yale University, New Haven, Conn., May.

Economist, "How Japan Cheapens the Yen." 19 November 1983, p. 77.

Edwards, Sebastian. 1983. "The Order of Liberalization of the Current and Capital Accounts of the Balance of Payments: A Survey of the Major Issues." Washington: World Bank.

Eken, Sena. "Integration of Domestic and International Financial Markets: The Japanese Experience." (Forthcoming, IMF *Staff Papers*.)

Engel, Charles, and Jeffrey Frankel. 1984. "Why Interest Rates React to Money Accouncements: An Explanation from the Foreign Exchange Market." *Journal of Monetary Economics*, January.

Feldstein, Martin. 1984. "The Dollar Exchange Rate." Remarks before the World Affairs Council of Philadelphia, 29 February.

Fox, Larry. 1984. "Testimony on the U.S. Trade Deficit" before the House Committee on Ways and Means, Subcommittee on Trade, 12 April.

Frankel, Jeffrey. 1982. "On the Franc." *Annales de l'INSEE*, pp. 47–48.

———. 1982. "In Search of the Exchange Risk Premium: A Six-Currency Test Assuming Mean-Variance Optimization." *Journal of International Money and Finance*, 1 December.

———. 1984. "The 1980–83 Dollar and Six Possible Meanings of 'Overvaluation'" July 1983. In *Floating Exchange Rates in an Interdependent World*, ed. Richard Cooper, et al. Washington: GAO, 20 April.

Freeman, Richard. 1984. "Aspects of Recent Japanese Financial Market Liberalization." Paper presented to Board of Governors of the Federal Reserve System, Conference at the Federal Reserve Bank of San Francisco, 11 May.

Frenkel, Jacob. 1981. "Flexible Exchange Rates, Prices, and the Role of 'News': Lessons from the 1970s." *Journal of Political Economy* 89, no. 4 (August): 665–705.

Friedland, Jonathan. 1984. "Experts Differ on Impact of Japanese Liberalization." *American Banker*, 12 June.

Fukao, Mitsuhiro. 1984. "International Ripple Effects of Interest Rates." *Economic Eye* 5, no. 1 (March): 12–17 (translated from *Shukan Toyo Keizai*, 18 November 1983).

General Accounting Office (GAO). 1984. *Floating Exchange Rates in an Interdependent World: No Simple Solutions to the Problems*. Washington, 20 April.

Hama, Atsushi. 1983. "The Yen-Dollar Relationship, Macroeconomic Policy, Financial and Capital Markets and Related Issues." *Keidanren Papers No. 10*, November.

Hamada, Koichi. 1984. "The Yen Problem and the Japanese Financial Market." Tokyo: University of Tokyo, 7 March.

Horiuchi, Akiyoshi. 1984. "Economic Growth and Financial Allocation in Postwar Japan." Brookings Discussion Papers in International Economics, no. 18, August.

International Monetary Fund. 1983. *Annual Report on Exchange Arrangements and Exchange Restrictions*. Washington.

Islam, Shafiqul. 1983–84. "Currency Misalignments: The Case of the Dollar and the Yen." *Federal Reserve Bank of New York Quarterly Review* 8, no. 4 (Winter): 49–60.

Ito, Takatoshi. 1983. "Capital Controls and Covered Interest Parity." NBER Working Paper no. 1187, August.

———. 1984. "Use of (Time-Domain) Vector Autoregressions to Test Uncovered Interest Parity." Minneapolis: University of Minnesota, September.

Iwata, Kazumata, and Koichi Hamada. 1980. *Kinyū seisaku to ginkō kōdō* ["Financial Policy and Bank Behavior"]. Tokyo: Tōyō Keizai Shimto Sha.

Japanese Economic Planning Agency. 1984. *The Japanese Economy Responding to New Internationalization*. Annual Economic Report to the Cabinet. Tokyo.

Japanese Ministry of Finance and US Department of the Treasury Working Group. 1984. *Report on Yen/Dollar Exchange Rate Issues*. Washington, May.

Kanemitsu, Hideo. 1983. "Comments." In *Trade Policy in the 1980s*, ed. William Cline. Washington: Institute for International Economics.

Katz, Richard. 1984. "The Financial Plan Behind the Regan-Takeshita Measures." *Diamond Weekly*, 3 March.

Kirkland, Richard. 1982. "Are the Japanese Rigging the Yen?" *Fortune*, 31 May, pp. 91–96.

Krugman, Paul. 1984. "The International Role of the Dollar: Theory and Prospect." In *Exchange Rate Theory and Practice* ed. J. Bilson and R. Marston, pp. 261–78. Chicago, Ill.: NBER, University of Chicago Press.

Look Japan. 1984. "Toward the Age of Full-Scale Financial Market Liberalization and Yen Internationalization: Interview with Tomomitsu Oba," and "MOF Reveals Landmark Recognition," 10 July.

McKinnon, Ronald. 1979. *Money in International Exchange: The Convertible Currency System*. New York: Oxford University Press.

———. 1983. "Dollar Overvaluation Against the Yen and Mark in 1983: How to Coordinate Central Bank Policies." *Aussenwirtschaft* 38 (January): 357–72.

———. 1983. "Financial Causes of Friction between Japan and the United States." In *The Future Course of US-Japan Economic Relations* ed. E. R. Fried, P. H. Tresize, and S. Yoshida. Washington: The Brookings Institution.

———. 1984. *An International Standard for Monetary Stabilization*. POLICY ANALYSES IN INTERNATIONAL ECONOMICS, no. 8. Washington: Institute for International Economics, March.

Muller, Patrice, and Robert Price. 1984. "Structural Budget Deficits and Fiscal Stance." OECD Economics and Statistics Department Working Paper no. 15, July.

Murchison, David, and Ezra Solomon. 1983. "The Misalignment of the United States Dollar and the Japanese Yen: The Problem and Its Solution." Unpublished, 19 September.

Niskanen, William. 1983. "Issues and Nonissues." In *The Future Course of US-Japan Economic Relations* ed. E. R. Fried, P. H. Tresize, and S. Yoshida. Washington: The Brookings Institution.

Organisation for Economic Cooperation and Development (OECD). 1984. *Economic Survey of Japan*, July.

———. 1984, *Economic Outlook* 35, July.

Otani, Ichiro. 1982. "Capital Markets in the 1980s: Potential for More Friction." In *U.S.-Japan Relations in the 1980s: Towards Border Sharing*. The Program on U.S.-Japan Relations. Cambridge, Mass.: Harvard University.

———. 1983. "Exchange Rate Instability and Capital Controls: The Japanese Experience 1978–81." In *Exchange Rate and Trade Instability: Causes, Consequences, and Remedies* ed. D. Bigman and T. Taya. Cambridge, Mass.: Ballinger.

Otani, Ichiro, and Siddarth Tiwari. 1981. "Capital Controls and Interest Rate Parity: The Japanese Experience 1978–81." *IMF Staff Papers*, December.

———. 1984. "Capital Controls, Interest Rate Policy, and Exchange Rates: A Theoretical Approach." Unpublished IMF paper, 23 May.

Pigott, Charles. 1983. "Financial Reform in Japan." *Federal Reserve Bank of San Francisco Economic Review* (Winter): 25–46.

Rowen, Hobart. 1984. "U.S., Japan Set Major Yen Accord." *Washington Post*, 30 May.

Rowley, Anthony. 1983. "The Reluctant Debutante." *Far Eastern Economic Review*, 29 December.

Sakakibara, Eisuke, and Akira Kondoh. 1984. *Study on the Internationalization of Tokyo's Money Markets*. Japan Center for International Finance Policy Study Series, no. 1, June.

Sato, Kazuo. 1982. "Japan's Savings and Internal and External Macroeconomic Balance." In *Policy and Trade Issues of the Japanese Economy* ed. Kozo Yamamura. Seattle: University of Washington Press.

Saxonhouse, Gary R. 1982. "Japanese Saving Behavior: A Household Balance Sheet Approach." Ann Arbor: University of Michigan, November.

———. 1983. "Tampering with Comparative Advantage in Japan?" Statement to US International Trade Commission. Washington, 15 June.

———. 1983. "The Micro- and Macroeconomics of Foreign Sales to Japan." In *Trade Policy in the 1980s* ed. William Cline, pp. 259–304. Washington: Institute for International Economics.

Solomon, Anthony. 1983. "External and Internal Balance in Japan's Financial Policies." In *The Future Course of U.S.-Japan Economic Relations* ed. E. R. Fried, P. H. Tresize, and S. Yoshida. Washington: The Brookings Institution.

Suzuki, Yoshio. 1984. "Financial Innovation and Monetary Policy in Japan." *Bank of Japan Monetary and Economic Studies* 2, no. 1 (June): 1–48.

United States–Japan Advisory Commission. 1984. *Challenges and Opportunities in United States–Japan Relations.* Report submitted to the President of the United States and the Prime Minister of Japan, September.

Williamson, John. 1983. *The Exchange Rate System.* POLICY ANALYSES IN INTERNATIONAL ECONOMICS, no. 5. Washington: Institute for International Economics, September.

World Financial Markets. 1984. "Japan's Financial Liberalization and Yen Internationalization." June.

Yellen, Thomas. 1984. "Why the Yen Will Under-Perform." *Euromoney* (June): 24–25.

Yoshitomi, Masaru. 1983. "An Analysis of Current Account Surpluses in the Japanese Economy." In *The Future Course of U.S.-Japan Economic Relations* ed. E.R. Fried, P.H. Tresize, and S. Yoshida. Washington: The Brookings Institution.

———. 1984. "Japan as Capital Exporter and the World Economy." Paper prepared for the Group of Thirty, 8 June.

———. 1984. "Japan's Viewpoint on the Current External Imbalance." Paper prepared for conference on "Imbalances in the World Economy: Macroeconomics, Structural Problems and Trade Policies." Washington: Institute for International Economics, 21–23 September.

INSTITUTE PUBLICATIONS

Title/Author/Publication Date/BOOK ORDERING CODE/Price

POLICY ANALYSES IN INTERNATIONAL ECONOMICS Series

1 *The Lending Policies of the International Monetary Fund*/John Williamson/August 1982/ WILPP/$6.00
2 *"Reciprocity": A New Approach to World Trade Policy?*/William R. Cline/September 1982/ CLIRP/$6.00
3 *Trade Policy in the 1980s*/C. Fred Bergsten and William R. Cline/November 1982/BERTP/ $6.00/Out of print but partially reproduced in chapter 22 in the book, *Trade Policy in the 1980s*.
4 *International Debt and the Stability of the World Economy*/William R. Cline/September 1983/CLIIP/$6.00
5 *The Exchange Rate System*/John Williamson/September 1983/WILEP/$6.00
6 *Economic Sanctions in Support of Foreign Policy Goals*/Gary Clyde Hufbauer and Jeffrey J. Schott/October 1983/HUFEP/$6.00
7 *A New SDR Allocation?*/John Williamson/March 1984/WILNP/$6.00
8 *An International Standard for Monetary Stabilization*/Ronald I. McKinnon/March 1984/ MCKNP/$6.00
9 *The Yen/Dollar Agreement: Liberalizing Japanese Capital Markets*/Jeffrey A. Frankel/ December 1984/FRAYP/$6.00

Forthcoming

Possible Modifications in International Bank Lending: The Alternatives and Their Implications/C. Fred Bergsten, William R. Cline, and John Williamson/January 1985/BERLP/$10.00
Deficits and the Dollar: The World Economy at Risk/Stephen Marris/February 1985/MARWP/ $6.00
Financial Intermediation Beyond the Debt Crisis/John Williamson/March 1985/WILFP/$6.00
International Trade in Automobiles: Liberalization or Further Restraint?/William R. Cline/ March 1985/CLINP/$6.00
The Next International Trade Negotiations/Gary Clyde Hufbauer and Jeffrey J. Schott/April 1985/HUFNP/$6.00
Reforming Trade Adjustment Policy/Gary Clyde Hufbauer and Howard F. Rosen/May 1985/ HUFRP/$6.00
The Multiple Reserve Currency System/C. Fred Bergsten and John Williamson/June 1985/ BERMP/$6.00
Another Multi-Fiber Arrangement?/William R. Cline/July 1985/CLIAP/$6.00
Second-Best Responses to Currency Misalignments/Stephen Marris/July 1985/MARSP/$6.00
Toward Cartelization of World Steel Trade?/William R. Cline/Fall 1985/CLITP/$6.00
New International Arrangements for Foreign Direct Investment/C. Fred Bergsten and Jeffrey J. Schott/Fall 1985/BERAP/$6.00

SPECIAL REPORTS

Promoting World Recovery/Twenty-six Economists/December 1982/TWEPP/$6.00/Out of print. See Order Information.
Prospects for Adjustment in Argentina, Brazil, and Mexico: Responding to the Debt Crisis/ John Williamson/WILAP/June 1983/$6.00/Out of print. See Order Information.

Forthcoming

Inflation and Indexation: Argentina, Brazil, and Israel/John Williamson, ed./WILP/February 1985/$8.00
Imbalances in the World Economy/C. Fred Bergsten, ed./?/March 1985/$6.00

BRIEFING MEMORANDA

The Trade and Tariff Act of 1984: A Description and Preliminary Assessment/Stephen L. Lande and Craig VanGrasstek/January 1985/LANAP/$10.00

BOOKS

IMF Conditionality/John Williamson, ed./1983/WILIH/$30.00 hardcover
Trade Policy in the 1980s/William R. Cline, ed./1983/CLIPH/$35.00 hardcover/CLIPP/$15.00 paper
International Debt: Systemic Risk and Policy Response/William R. Cline/1984/CLITH/$25.00
Subsidies in International Trade/Gary Clyde Hufbauer and Joanna Shelton Erb/1984/HUFSH/$30.00 hardcover

Forthcoming

Economic Sanctions Reconsidered: History and Current Policy/Gary Clyde Hufbauer and Jeffrey J. Schott/February 1985/HUFEH/$45.00 hardcover
Domestic Adjustment and International Trade/Gary Clyde Hufbauer and Howard F. Rosen/Winter 1985/HUFDH/$25.00 hardcover
Trade Controls in Three Industries/William R. Cline/Fall 1985/CLICH/$25.00 hardcover
International Coordination of National Economic Policies/Stephen Marris/Winter 1985/MAROH/$30.00 hardcover

---

ORDER INFORMATION

- Books in print can be purchased from your local bookseller or from MIT Press, 28 Carleton Street, Cambridge, Mass. 02142.
- Books out of print can be purchased from Books on Demand, University Microfilm International, 300 North Zeeb Road, Ann Arbor, Mich. 48106 (telephone 313-761-4700).
- Standing orders for all publications or for POLICY ANALYSES only are invited from companies, institutions, and libraries in the United States and Canada. Write MIT Press for information.
- Orders from individuals must be accompanied by payment in US dollars, credit card number, or request for a proforma invoice.
- Prices outside the United States and Canada are slightly higher. Write MIT Press for a proforma invoice.

ORDER FORM

Please open a standing order for

☐ All forthcoming titles.

☐ All forthcoming POLICY ANALYSES.

☐ All forthcoming titles and all past titles still in print.

Please send only:

Title/Author	*Book Code*	*Price*

POSTAGE

Domestic: Book rate $1.50 each hardcover; $0.75 each paper. First class $3.50 each hardcover; $2.50 each paper.

Foreign: Surface $0.75 each paper; $1.75 each hardcover. Airmail $8.00 each hardcover; $3.00 each paper.

Postage _____

TOTAL US$ _____

PAYMENT

☐ Purchase order attached.

☐ Check enclosed (drawn to MIT Press).

Charge to ☐ Mastercard ☐ Visa

Card number _____ Expiration date _____

(Minimum credit card order $10.00)

Ship to

NAME _____

Please print   First   Middle   Last

AFFILIATION _____

ADDRESS   CITY _____

STATE OR PROVINCE   POSTAL CODE   COUNTRY